CRIME SCENE USA

A Traveler's Guide to the Locations of Famous and Infamous Murders, Robberies, Kidnappings, and Other Unlawful Acts

From The Bureau of Amateur Detectives and Gatherers of Evidence (BADGE)

by Neal S. Yonover

ABOUT THE CONTRIBUTORS

The Bureau of Amateur Detectives and Gatherers of Evidence (BADGE) is a national organization dedicated to the preservation of crime scenes past and present. Formed in 1983 by a group of average citizens who were all the victims of unsolved crimes, BADGE's mission is to research, identify, and promote awareness of the sites of crimes solved and unsolved in the United States. Members of BADGE prefer to remain anonymous, but include ex-policemen, private detectives, housewives, lawyers, doctors, and others from all walks of life.

Disclaimer: The views expressed in this book are those of the Authors. The Publisher does not endorse the Authors' views, nor does the Publisher express any opinion on the veracity of any of the material and information presented by the Authors.

ISBN: 0-7868-8397-9

First Edition
10 9 8 7 6 5 4 3 2 1

TABLE OF CONTENTS

INTRODUCTION

> "I don't mind a reasonable amount of trouble."—Sam Spade
>
> "And hey! Let's be careful out there."
> —Sergeant Esterhaus, *Hill Street Blues*

Welcome to the scene of the crime—wherever you happen to be. If you aren't standing at a crime scene right now, don't worry. They're just like buses. One will be along in a few minutes. Even though we know crime doesn't pay, and that the weed of crime does indeed bear bitter fruit, we are, as a nation, fascinated by crime.

We watch crime on TV, see it at the movies, read about it, surf it on the 'net, and slow down for it when we're driving. Without crime, the Discovery Channel, A&E, Court TV, the self-styled "news" magazine shows, and most of the networks would be broadcasting test patterns about 18 hours a day. From *America's Most Wanted* to *America's Dumbest Criminals*, our desire for information about lawbreakers, scofflaws, crimefighters, miscreants, and perpetrators is insatiable. We even tour old prisons and sing about crime. Based on the broadcast ratings for events like O.J. Simpson's low-speed chase or Court TV in general, we have always been intrigued by, well, intrigue.

The bottom line, as one true crime fan described it, is that "The place where Lincoln gave the Gettysburg address is interesting, but not like the place where he was shot. Because it's history, only better."

Crime Scene USA is your guide to the most dramatic, most compelling crimes in the country. With the help of an army of reference librarians, the actual law enforcement professionals who investigated the crimes, state tourism professionals, museum curators, and other experts who generously shared their time and knowledge (no matter how bizarre the request), we have shaken the nation's information resources like a giant piggy bank until every single shiny detail of the most fascinating true crime locations popped out. And they're all here.

Within, you'll find the sites of crimes present and past, from Old West shoot-outs to serial killing-sprees, from infamous incidents to today's tabloid crimes, not to mention prison tours, crime-oriented museums, mafia hangouts, the sites of famous assassinations, and even a few criminal hometowns. At each site you can learn the story of the crime—what, where, when, how, why, and whodunit.

With this book to guide you, you can visit the sites of more than a hundred notorious crimes throughout the nation that you've heard about in the news and read about for years, armed with the inside knowledge of an investigating detective. You'll be able to see for yourself how the crime itself played out—state by state. Who knows? You might even solve a few.

Either way, enjoy your trip—and don't forget your fingerprint kit.

THE CRIME SCENE VISITOR'S GUIDE

To derive maximum value from the crime scenes listed in this book, here are some helpful tips.

1. Don't go to the crime scene unless you're prepared. Make sure you have your copy of *Crime Scene USA* in hand, with the proper sections bookmarked.

2. Bring a camera or video recording equipment. Producing your own crime scene footage may reveal entirely new insight into the crime.

3. Do not bring anything that remotely resembles a weapon to the scene of a crime. Even though the crime may not have occurred recently, there are probably still a few exposed nerves—especially for those in law enforcement.

4. Keep your eyes open as you visit the crime scenes in this book. You never know who might be standing around the corner.

5. With few exceptions, the most vicious sociopathic killers look just like everyone else. If we didn't know who and what they were, we'd all walk right past people like John Wayne Gacy, Jeffrey Dahmer, and Ted Bundy on the street without even noticing them. You may already know the next notorious serial killer.

6. Serial killers **do** return to the scene of the crime (not out of guilt, but to relive the thrill).

7. Respect private property. Do not trespass—you might end up sharing a cell with a present (or future) *Crime Scene USA* perp.

Welcome to the scene of the crime.

LEGEND

KIDNAPPINGS

MURDERS AND ATTEMPTED MURDERS

ORGANIZED CRIME

ROBBERIES

SERIAL KILLERS

SPIES

UNBELIEVABLE CRIME

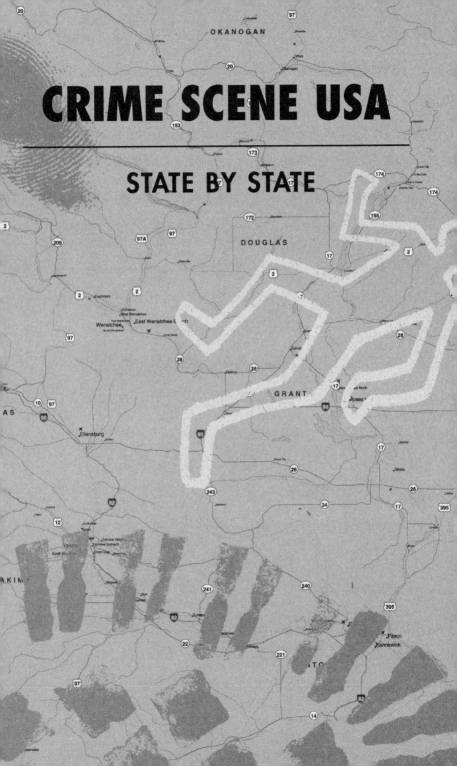

CRIME SCENE USA

STATE BY STATE

Alabama

Alabama is a very colorful state. The state's electric chair is known as "Yellow Mama." Yellow because the only paint they had when the first chair was built in 1923 was yellow highway paint; Mama because, in the words of an Alabama State Correctional Department spokesman, "Everybody goes home to Mama"—especially from this lethal lap.

Welcome to the Heart of Dixie, crime scene fans.

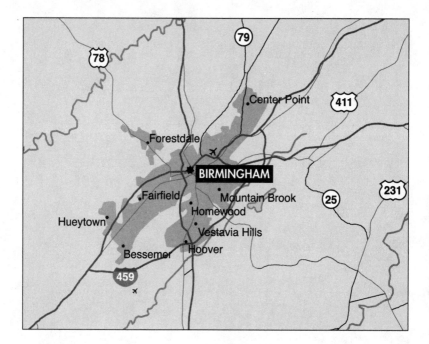

BIRMINGHAM

THE STORY: *"White Supremacists Blow Up Church,*
Kill 4 Young Women"—1963

September 15, 1963, began as a very ordinary Sunday morning at the **16th Street Baptist Church**. Everyone was in their Sunday best. Denise McNair, age 11, and Carole Robertson, Cynthia

Wesley, and Addie Mae Collins, all age 14, were crowded into the women's lounge in the basement of the church, primping before start of the 11:00 A.M. service. The church was planning to introduce a series of monthly youth Sundays, to celebrate the younger members of the congregation.

Moments later, several sticks of dynamite exploded, killing all four young women in the lounge. The horrified reaction to the murders, and worldwide condemnation of racial violence, made this crime one of the turning points in the civil rights movement.

In 1977, the only person who was ever charged in the case, Robert Chambliss, was convicted. He died in prison in 1985. In 1997, the FBI and the Birmingham police announced that they had reopened the investigation.

The church was rebuilt and became a milestone in the civil rights trail.

In 1997, director Spike Lee made *4 Little Girls*, a documentary about the bombing.

THE SCENE:

16th Street Baptist Church
1530 Sixth Avenue North
Birmingham, AL

Calling All Cars! Major Museum Alert!

Birmingham's Civil Rights District
Kelly Ingram Park
Sixth Avenue North at 16th Street
Birmingham, AL

Across the street from the church is Kelly Ingram Park, a historical "Place of Revolution and Reconciliation," and the site of grassroots resistance to discrimination.

The paths of the park lead visitors through three-dimensional sculptures that commemorate the sentiments of the 1960s and recreate what the marchers experienced: police dogs and firehoses. All paths on Freedom Walk converge on the park's center, a peaceful and meditative life-spring of hope.

MONTGOMERY

THE STORY: *"Waitress Poisons 7, Is Last Woman Executed in State"—1956*

 If only she'd received better tips.... Forty-nine-year-old Rhonda Bell Martin was a waitress in Montgomery who discovered a useful formula: poison relatives, collect insurance money. Insurance claims followed the deaths of her mother, two of her five husbands (the last one survived, but was paralyzed from the waist down), and two of her children (two more died under what investigators termed "unusual" circumstances).

She received the death sentence and was executed in the electric chair on October 11, 1957. She stands as the last woman to sit in Yellow Mama's lap.

THE SCENE:

Old Kilby Prison (now Montgomery Industrial Park)
Off Congressman Dickinson Boulevard at Newell Parkway
Near Gunner Air Force Base
Montgomery, AL

Yellow Mama and the state's Death Row were moved from Old Kilby Prison in Montgomery to the Holman Correctional Institution in Atmore in 1968. An industrial park is on the Old Kilby site today.

Calling All Cars! Museum Alert!

Pauly Jail Museum
217-½ North Prairie Street (behind the courthouse)
Union Springs, AL 36089
334-738-TOUR

Built in 1897, the jail still has a working trapdoor for hangings and a portable jail (city officials bought a traveling circus's lion cage after the lion died).

Alaska

The "Last Frontier" has a criminal history that's as colorful as it is remote. Alaska has crimes even the legendary radio and TV crime-fighting Canadian Mountie, Sgt. Preston, and his wonder dog, Yukon King, couldn't solve—though they're just as engrossing to read about.

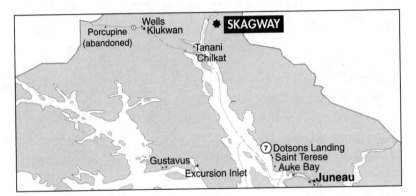

SKAGWAY

THE STORY: *"Crime Kingpin Dies in Shoot-out"—1898*

 Skagway, which means "Home of the North Wind," was the gateway to the Klondike Gold Rush. Thousands of frenzied gold-hunters passed through this boomtown en route to their dreams. Without any semblance of law, the town was known in archived reports from the time as "the most outrageously lawless quarter on the globe."

The great bad-man of the time was Jefferson Randall Smith, known as "Soapy." Smith was a ruthless con artist from Colorado who ran all the fraud, theft, armed robbery, and murders in town. He also had a secret spy network and army of thugs to enforce his wishes.

On July 8, 1898, Smith was shot by Frank Reid, the surveyor who plotted out the town, when Smith tried to crash a meeting of the town's vigilance committee. Smith, 38, died instantly. Reid died an agonizing week later from a wound to the groin. Reid's gravestone reads, "He gave his life for the honor of Skagway."

Today, the town still has many of the boardwalks, frontier seafronts, and other artifacts from those days.

Soapy Smith's demise and Skagway's bad old days are commemorated every July 8 with a wake held at the cemetery. Smith's grandson lives in Southern California and comes up annually for the event. A show based on Soapy Smith's rule in Skagway, "The Days of '98," is performed nightly at the Eagle's Hall saloon theater. Staged for over 65 years, it is the longest-running show in Alaska.

THE SCENES:

Soapy Smith's Parlor
Across Broadway on 2nd Street
Skagway, AK

Soapy Smith's and Frank Reid's grave markers
(Reid has the largest monument, while Smith only rated a wooden plank.)
Gold Rush Cemetery
Skagway, AK
Two miles north of town, beside the railroad tracks

FOR MORE INFORMATION:

Skagway Convention and Visitor Bureau
907-983-2854

Calling All Cars! Museum Alert!

Fraternal Order of Alaska State Trooper Museum
320 West Fifth Avenue, Suite 136
(Anchorage Fifth Avenue Mall—Street Level)
P.O. Box 100280
Anchorage, AK 99510
800-770-5050

The museum and store are just two blocks east of Anchorage's Egan Convention Center. Access is from Sixth Avenue Street Level, right across the street from Nordstrom's. Hours are from 10:00 to 4:00 weekdays and 12:00 to 4:00 on Saturday.

Arizona

Primarily known for its preserved Western outlaw heritage with land-marks such as the city of Tombstone and the OK Corral, the state also has its share of more modern crimes and criminals.

Modern crime and prison history have converged here in the Grand Canyon State. Today, the Maricopa County Sheriff is running a low-budget, no-frills, tent-city prison that harkens back to the old Yuma Territorial Prison days. It's also a harsh place designed to discourage repeat visits. The sheriff does have a sense of humor, though. The Vacancy sign out front is lit all the time.

Read All About It!

Clues Unlimited Mystery/Crime Bookstore
123 South Eastbourne Drive #16
Tucson, AZ 85716
520-326-8533
Fax: 520-326-9001
clues@azstarnet.com
www.cluesunlimited.com

BISBEE

THE STORY: *"'Mormon Bill' and the Bisbee Massacre"—1883*

 On December 8, itinerant bartender, miner, and killer William "Mormon Bill" Delaney and a group of other vicious outlaws rode into town, held up the Castaneda-Goldwater store, and killed five people—including a woman—before escaping. A month later he was captured in Mexico and brought back to Tombstone, where he was quickly convicted and hanged. On hearing the sentence, Delaney boasted, "No man will stand [the hanging] better than I." At the gallows on March 3, 1884, he proved it. None did.

THE SCENE:

Bisbee Massacre Site
24 to 26 Main Street
Bisbee, AZ

* * * * * *

THE STORY: *"First Union Strike Thwarted by Management"—1917*

 Protesting members of the IWW (Industrial Workers of the World, known as the Wobblies) staged a strike at the **Phelps-Dodge Copper Mining Company**. Rather than negotiate, on July 12, 1917, the mine's management had Sheriff Harry Wheeler organize a 1,000-man posse (essentially one-third of the town) and seize more than 2,000 striking workers (the rest of the town) in a pre-dawn raid. He marched them to **Warren Ballpark**, forced them into waiting cattle cars, and shipped them across the state line into New Mexico, effectively breaking the IWW. The mine was so powerful that the local courts would not permit any legal action to be filed against the firm.

THE SCENES:

Phelps-Dodge Copper Mining Company
36 West Highway 92
Bisbee, AZ

Warren Ballpark
On Douglas Road at the south
  end of Vista Park Road
Bisbee, AZ

Sentence Yourself To a Night in Jail

The OK Street Jailhouse Inn
9 OK Street
P.O. Box 1152
Bisbee, AZ 85603
800-821-0678
520-432-7435
Fax: 520-432-7434

A jail from 1904 to 1915 that reinforced law and order in this booming mining town, the two-story building has been remodeled into a fully furnished apartment suite which is available as a private rental.

The first floor jailer's office is now a small sitting area. The drunk tank houses the living room, kitchen, and bath. And the second floor cells, originally for serious offenders, offer sitting rooms, a bedroom, and full bathrooms.

The jail still has its original heavy metal doors, which sometimes stick. When that happens, though, instead of a locksmith, they call a slick attorney to get you out.

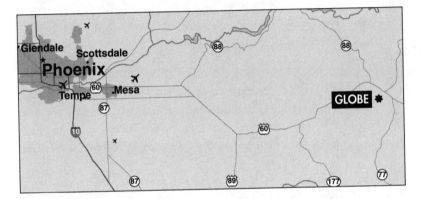

GLOBE

THE STORY: *"Pearl Hart, the West's Only Female Stagecoach Robber"—1899*

 Unlike other lady outlaws of the day, such as Belle Starr or Cattle Kate Watson, Pearl Hart was born into a respectable, middle-class family in Ontario, Canada, and attended finishing school. Despite the refinements, Pearl was fascinated by the legends of the Wild West and moved to Arizona to join them in the early 1890s.

Hart entered the ranks of Western outlaw history in 1899 when she robbed the Globe Florence Stagecoach at gunpoint to get money for her ailing mother. Even though it was the criminal equivalent of taking candy from a baby because the stagecoach had been rendered all but obsolete by the westward expansion of the railroad, it was good enough for the record books.

The robbery was successful, but the escape wasn't. Hart and her partner, Joe Boot, promptly got themselves lost galloping off into the hills.

They were surrounded by the posse the next morning, awakened, and escorted back to the **Gila County Jail and Courthouse** in Globe. Nonetheless, Pearl Hart had achieved outlaw sensation: she was the first woman in recorded history to hold up a stagecoach and the last Western bandit to do so.

THE SCENE:

Old Gila County Jail and Courthouse
(now the Cobre Valley Center for the Arts)
100 North Broad Street
Globe, AZ

Built in 1908, with cellblocks from the Yuma Territorial Facility, the jail is located behind the Old Globe County Courthouse. Criminals were shuffled between the two buildings via a second-floor walkway. The jail held prisoners until 1978. It now houses the Cobre Valley Center for the Arts.

For more information:
The Greater Globe-Miami Chamber of Commerce
520-425-4495

Stop in for a Shot at the Bucket of Blood Saloon

The Bucket of Blood Saloon
On South East Central Street at Navajo
Holbrook, AZ

Originally known as The Cottage, this saloon in Holbrook was a popular Saturday night hangout for cowboys with the rough-and-tumble Hashknife cattle outfit. One night Joe Crawford, a former Hashknife employee, settled a gambling disagreement by killing everyone at the table. He was also wounded. One spectator described the scene as looking like someone had spilled a bucket of blood, and the name stuck. The saloon was so notorious that it prevented the establishment of a church in Holbrook for 36 years.

Arkansas

Arkansas was the mecca for Southern-style crime long before the Whitewater investigation.

Hot Springs was the Mob Riviera, with drinking, gambling, and prostitution widely available until 1963. During the Westward Expansion, Fort Smith was the last civilization, i.e., the last place with courthouse and brothels, for thousands of miles.

Welcome to the Natural State, y'all.

HOT SPRINGS

THE STORY: *"Exiled Crime Boss Turns Hot Springs into Little Las Vegas"—1937*

Known as "The Duke" to most people for his courtly ways, Owen "Owney" Madden owned much of New York City in the 1920s, including legendary speakeasies and nightclubs like The Stork Club and the Cotton Club. He was one of Mae West's lovers and got his

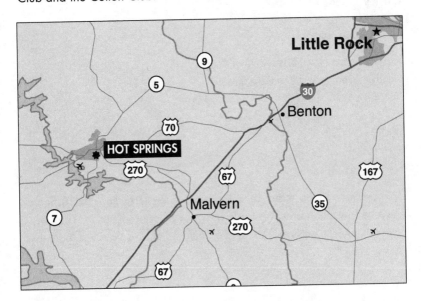

boyhood friend George Raft into movies. Raft's "Rinaldo" character in *Scarface* is modeled after Madden, right down to the tilt of his hat.

In 1935, when things got too hot in Manhattan, Madden exiled himself to Hot Springs, where he flourished in congenial corruption. Within months of his arrival, he married the local postmaster's daughter, moved into a huge white mansion and opened a gambling house, **The Southern Club**, across from the stately **Arlington Hotel**. The Arlington was a hangout for gangsters from all over the country, where they came to enjoy the pleasures afforded by the neutral "Switzerland" of crime. Like Las Vegas, there was no "business" conducted in town and everybody was safe there—from arrest and other gangsters.

How powerful was Madden? Arkansas was a dry state until 1970, yet you could openly buy a drink and gamble in any of his clubs until 1963.

A political crackdown on Hot Springs gambling finally put Madden out of business in 1964. He died a year later, on April 24, 1965.

The "Dave the Dude" character in Damon Runyon's *Guys and Dolls* is patterned after him.

THE SCENES:

Owney Madden's House
506 West Grand Avenue
Hot Springs, AR

The Arlington Hotel Resort Hotel & Spa
Central Avenue and Fountain Street
P.O. Box 5652
Hot Springs National Park, AR 71902
800-643-1502
501-623-7771
Fax: 501-623-2243

In addition to its many other charms, gangsters liked **The Arlington** because it allowed an unobstructed view of all approaches. Al Capone, a frequent guest, always took the whole floor and always stayed in room 442.

The Gables Inn B&B
318 Quapaw Avenue
Hot Springs National Park, AR 71901
800-625-7576
501-623-7576
gablesinn@ipa.net

A three-part mystery dinner evening in conjunction with "The Belle of Hot Springs" paddlewheeler and Gilligan's Island restaurant.

Crime Scene Calendar Alert!!!

Showdown At Sunset
Union County Courthouse Square
P.O. Box 1325
El Dorado, AR 71730
888-921-BOOM

The annual re-creation of a fierce gunfight that occurred on October 2, 1902, and left three men dead and several others wounded, including City Marshal Guy B. Tucker, grandfather of former Arkansas Governor Jim Guy Tucker.

According to the legend, the Tuckers and the Parnells were feuding over many things, the least of which were land and a romantic triangle between the families. Even after the gunfight, the dispute lasted until 1905.

"A psychotic thinks 2 and 2 are 5. A normal person knows 2 and 2 are 4. A neurotic knows 2 and 2 are 4, but can't stand it. And a psychopath knows 2 and 2 are 4 or 6 or 71 or 800, depending on what he thinks you WANT him to believe, because he's just putting on a show, an appearance."

—Jack Olsen, best-selling crime writer, author of over thirty crime books

The Old Fort Museum
320 Rogers Avenue
Fort Smith, AR 72901
501-783-7841
Fax: 501-783-7848

In 1875, Judge Isaac C. Parker was the last law before Indian Territory. His rigid interpretation of Frontier Justice in more than 13,000 cases over 21 years made him known as "The Hanging Judge" for the 151 men he sent to the gallows. Only 79 were actually hanged. The others remained in prison until they were paroled or died.

Stand in his courtroom here in the Old Fort Museum and you can almost hear him pronouncing sentences.

The book and Academy Award-winning movie *True Grit* is based on Parker and his group of deputized lawmen. John Wayne's "Rooster Cogburn" character was one of them.

It Would Be a Crime if You Missed . . .

Miss Laura's Social Club
(now known as Miss Laura's Visitors' Center)
2 North B Street
Fort Smith, AR
800-637-1477

The sign could have read: "Last Sex for 1,000 Miles!" because Miss Laura's was the last bordello before Indian Territory. Though there were many brothels in the bustling Front Street area known as "The Row," Miss Laura's was the most refined. Her establishment featured song, dance, and chilled champagne, in addition to the less-than-legal pleasures to be found upstairs.

Today, the building is the only former bordello on the National Register of Historic Places. Amazingly, the building is still a destination for weary travelers looking for entertainment—the strictly legal kind. Today, it houses the Fort Smith Convention and Visitors' Bureau. They can't direct you to any real brothels, but they will help you find good restaurants and other local attractions.

California

Welcome to the serial killer state. Have a nice day.

What is it about this place that makes it such a Golden State for bad deeds?

The weather and climate are stultifyingly beautiful and yet the place probably has the highest per capita serial killer incidence in the nation and twice as many cases of serial killing than any other state.

But what's bad for California is good for us—suffice it to say that the entire state is rife with crime scenes.

ALCATRAZ ISLAND, SAN FRANCISCO BAY

THE STORY: *"Society's Most Vicious Felons Make Alcatraz Island Their Home"—1934*

Even though it's Spanish for "albatross," the word that embodies this island prison in the middle of the San Francisco Bay is "isolation." From the time it opened as a federal facility in 1934 during the violent 1930s gangster era until the last boatload of prisoners left on March 21, 1963, Alcatraz was specifically designed to do one thing: isolate America's most notorious criminals. As a warehouse for the safekeeping, not rehabilitation, of the nation's toughest convicts, it was the home (far) away from everyone else's home for kidnappers, racketeers, and other societal predators.

The Rock's remoteness also made it impossible for "connected" criminals like Al Capone to run his empire from prison because he couldn't have the daily contact with his "family" members as he'd had in Atlanta's federal pen.

In addition to Capone, the list of Rock "stars" who stayed here included George "Machine Gun" Kelly, the bootlegger who graduated to bank robberies after studying with the greats housed at Leavenworth; Robert "Birdman of Alcatraz" Stroud; and Alvin "Creepy" Karpis, Charles Manson's guitar teacher, a 26-year resident.

The prison's isolation, plus the cold water and ruthless bay tides,

ALCATRAZ ISLAND—THE ROCK, TO ITS FRIENDS.

proved an effective deterrent to escapes. Of the thirty-six who tried, only two prisoners are known to have made the swim across the bay. Both were grateful to be picked up as they stepped out of the hypothermia-inducing water.

In June 1962, however, Frank Morris, a Louisiana bank robber with an IQ of 133 and a history of landlocked prison escapes, led Florida bank robbers John and Clarence Anglin in an escape that may have been successful. The trio used spoons to dig their way out of their cells on the first tier of the triple-tiered B cell block and left dummies in their beds made from plaster with hair from the prison barbershop to fool guards. They made their way up through the roof and out to the water, where they used driftwood and pontoons made from raincoats to make a raft. The raft and the remains of their escape tools were all that were ever found. A San Francisco police officer reported seeing a strange fishing boat in the Bay early on the morning after the escape.

According to the Coast Guard, the tides on the night of the escape would have pushed the convicts away from San Francisco, toward the Marin shore. Soon after the escape, the *San Francisco Chronicle* reported the theft of an automobile in Marin County. A motorist reported that he'd been forced off the road by the car, which he said contained three men.

Since they were never found or caught, the three could still be at large. Here is how they were described in the *San Francisco Chronicle* on June 13, 1962, two days after their escape.

FRANK LEE MORRIS, age 35, height 5-7 ½, weight 135 pounds, hazel eyes, black hair, with these tattoos: a devil's head on upper right arm, a star on each knee (the one on the left knee has a "7" above and an "11" below), a star at the base of the left thumb, the number "13" at the base of the left index finger.

JOHN ANGLIN, age 32, height 5-10, weight 140 pounds, blue eyes, blond hair, medium build, small scar on left cheek, round scar on left forearm.

CLARENCE ANGLIN, age 31, height 5-11, weight 168 pounds, hazel eyes, light complexion, "Zona" tattooed on left wrist, "Nita" on right forearm.

Clint Eastwood played Frank Morris in the 1979 movie *Escape From Alcatraz*.

THE SCENE:

Alcatraz Federal Prison (a national park)
San Francisco, CA
To order tickets ahead of time, call 415-705-5555.
For group reservations, call 415-705-8214.
The tour boat leaves from Pier 41, Fisherman's Wharf.

There are bookstores both on the dock and in the cellhouse where you can buy all types of memorabilia and **Alcatraz Island** souvenirs.

BERKELEY

THE STORY: *"Kidnapped Heiress Becomes Revolutionary, Bank Robber"—1974*

 On February 4, 1974, a woman knocked on the door of **Patricia Hearst and Steven Weed's Berkeley duplex.** As soon as the door opened, two men with semi-automatic weapons forced their way in. They beat Weed severely and

dragged Hearst from the apartment, dumping her in the trunk of their stolen car and driving away after shooting at onlookers drawn by the commotion.

Patty Hearst, granddaughter of media baron William Randolph Hearst (whose life inspired the movie *Citizen Kane*), had been kidnapped by members of the Symbionese Liberation Army (SLA).

For the next twenty months Hearst's odyssey dominated the media. On April 3, the world heard an audiotape in which Patty Hearst renounced her life as an heiress and announced that she had taken the name "Tania," after a revolutionary who'd fought alongside Che Guevara, and become a freedom fighter in the SLA.

On the morning of April 15, the **Hibernia Bank** was robbed by machine-gun-toting men and women who made off with $10,000. The surveillance tape showed a heavily armed "Tania," in a dark wig and coat, taking a prominent role in the holdup.

Patty Hearst was branded a "common criminal" by investigators, and the womanhunt continued. Using the address from a parking ticket found in an abandoned SLA getaway van, FBI agents and SWAT teams swarmed around the SLA headquarters in Watts. A gunfight ensued and the house soon caught fire. Citing the danger, police refused to let firefighters battle the flames. Six SLA members died in the blaze, the entire Symbionese Liberation Army except Patty Hearst and William Harris, another SLA member, who watched the house burn from their hotel room nearby.

Hearst and Harris spent the next year underground, enjoying the hospitality of a network of 1960s radicals. On September 18, 1975, Harris, Hearst, and several others were captured in **San Francisco**. A handcuffed Hearst did her best to flash a power fist salute to reporters as she was escorted to jail.

From "Tania" to "Defendant." On March 11, 1976, despite a spirited defense by celebrity trial lawyer F. Lee Bailey (see Boston, Massachusetts), who claimed that Hearst had been brainwashed and coerced by the SLA, Hearst was convicted of robbing the Hibernia Bank. She received a seven-year sentence. Hearst's new moniker became Prisoner 00077-181 in the Federal Correctional Facility at Pleasanton, California.

On February 1, 1979, her sentence was commuted by President Jimmy Carter to time served on the basis that the abuse she endured at the

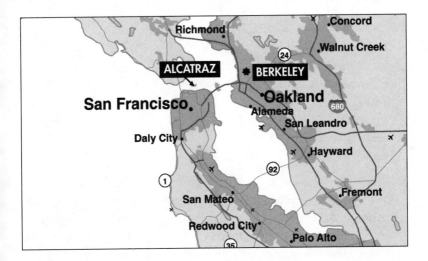

hands of her captors caused her to commit the crimes.

Shortly after her release, Hearst married and had two daughters. In addition to rejoining the society scene, where she uses her notoriety to help raise funds for charities and public causes, Hearst has also enjoyed an acting career, with small parts in director John Waters' films *Cry Baby* (1990), *Serial Mom* (1994), and *Pecker* (1998).

Hearst has also enjoyed a career as a writer. She wrote her memoir, *Every Secret Thing* (1982) and *Patty Hearst: Her Own Story* with Alvin Moscow in 1988. Hearst tried her hand at fiction in 1996 with *Murder at San Simeon (First Love No. 102)* with co-authors Martha Humphreys and Cordelia Frances Biddle.

THE SCENES:

Patty Hearst and Steven Weed's Duplex
1602 Benvenue
Berkeley, CA

The Hibernia Bank (Sunset District Office)
1450 Noriega Street
San Francisco, CA

Patty Hearst Capture Site
625 Morse Street
San Francisco, CA

Escape Artist Tours, Inc.
150 Tiller Court
Half Moon Bay, CA 94019
650-726-7626
Fax: 650-726-7647
eat@sf-escapes.com
www.sf-escapes.com

Crime doesn't have to be unpleasant. Escape Artist Tours, Inc. can make a custom murder-mystery weekend for your family, your office, or group of friends in which everyone gets their own part in the drama. More interactive than any staged mystery, they will make all the necessary arrangements, including finding a hotel or bed-and-breakfast in the San Francisco Bay area to accommodate your weekend. Contact them to set it all up!

BEVERLY HILLS

THE STORY: *"The Manson Family Murders"—1969*

 During a weeklong killing spree, a group of Charles Martin Manson's "family" broke into the **home of actress Sharon Tate**, 26, wife of director Roman Polanski. They butchered Tate, who was several months pregnant at the time, Abigail Folger, Jay Sebring, and two others in the hope that it would ignite a race riot and please Manson. The killers wrote "Helter Skelter," the title of a Beatles' song on the *White* album, on the walls of the house with their victims' blood. They later broke into **the house of Leno and Rosemary LaBianca**, torturing and killing them too.

Vincent Bugliosi, prosecutor for the murder trial, wrote *Helter Skelter: The True Story of the Manson Murders* with Curt Gentry in 1974. The best-selling book made a killing and allowed for memoirs by anyone connected with a notorious case, a trend which reached its peak after the O.J. Simpson trial (see Los Angeles) when the 6-year-old daughter of a woman who watched the televised trial published her story.

The entire Manson family was later arrested at their "home" on the **Spahn Ranch**, an old Western movie backlot. The rundown ranch had become the home for transients and runaways. Manson was found trying to hide in a bathroom cabinet. He was convicted of masterminding the murders and now resides at the **Corcoran Correctional Facility** along with other criminal VIPs such as Robert F. Kennedy's killer, Sirhan Sirhan, mass murderer Juan Corona, and others.

THE SCENES:

Sharon Tate's House
10050 Cielo Drive
Beverly Hills, CA

**Leno and Rosemary
LaBianca's House**
3301 Waverly
Los Angeles, CA

Spahn Ranch
12000 Santa Susana Pass Road
San Fernando Valley, CA

Corcoran Correctional Facility
4001 King Avenue
Corcoran, CA

* * * * * *

THE STORY: *"Gangster Bugsy Siegel Dies in Hail of Bullets"—1947*

 Popularized by Warren Beatty's award-winning 1991 movie *Bugsy*, this is the house where Siegel's career as a celebrity criminal came to a violent, bloody end. The killer who built the Flamingo Hotel (reportedly naming it after his girlfriend, Virginia Hill, known as "The Flamingo") and eventually transformed Las Vegas into a gambling mecca, was shotgunned to death while sitting in **Hill's living room**.

The blasts, which virtually decapitated him, were believed to have been caused by blatant refusal to repay the millions Lucky Luciano had loaned for the construction of the Flamingo. Virginia Hill, who was out of the country at the time of the murder, was later called by a congressional committee to testify about the mob in 1951. Hill was found dead on a mountaintop in Austria on March 14, 1966. A 1996 Associated Press story in the *Las Vegas Sun* reported that while her death was ruled a suicide, there were some that believed the mob was responsible because they were worried about what she knew.

THE SCENES:

Virginia Hill's House
810 Linden Drive
Beverly Hills, CA

Beth Olam Mausoleum
Beth Olam Cemetery
900 North Gower Street
Los Angeles, CA

Siegel's body lies in the **mausoleum at Beth Olam Cemetery**. Use the entrance near Gower Street. Turn right at the second aisle. His crypt is on the left, near the middle of section 2, third row from the bottom.

TOMB IT MAY CONCERN

Andrew Cunanan
Serial killer; murdered fashion designer Gianni Versace and four others. Holy Cross Mausoleum in the Holy Rosary Chapel, 6 crypts up from the floor in the niche area.

Holy Cross Cemetery
4470 Hilltop Drive
San Diego, California

LOS ANGELES

THE STORY: *"The Black Dahlia"—1947*

 On January 15, 1947, the halves of a nude young woman's body were found in the weeds of a lover's lane. Later identified as Elizabeth "Betty" Short, 22, a waitress, aspiring actress, and Hollywood party girl known as "The Black Dahlia" for her artfully arranged jet-black dyed hair and her penchant for black clothing.

An autopsy later revealed that she'd been tied up and brutally tortured for several days. The killer dissected her body, drained it of blood, washed the pieces, carefully set her hair and arranged the pieces in the empty lot where they were found.

While the crime is officially unsolved, Detective Joel Lesnick of the L.A. County Sheriff's Department and legendary LAPD Detective "Jigsaw" John St. John both came to the conclusion that Short was killed by Jack

Anderson Wilson, a tall, gaunt alcoholic with a crippled leg and a history of sex offenses and robbery. They also suspected Wilson of the similarly heinous murder of a Los Angeles socialite. Before they could pursue the case further, Wilson burned to death in a hotel fire he caused when he passed out in bed with a lit cigarette. The flames also consumed any possible evidence.

THE SCENE:

The Black Dahlia's body discovery site:
3925 South Norton Avenue (between Coliseum and 39th)
Los Angeles, CA

THE STORY: *"The O.J. Simpson Murder Case"—1995*

In the recent Crime of the Century, with a subsequent Trial of the Century, Nicole Brown Simpson, divorced wife of football star O.J. Simpson, and her friend Ron Goldman were killed in a brutal commando-style knife attack in front of **Ms. Simpson's condo** on June 13, 1994. Goldman, who was in the wrong place at the wrong time, was reportedly merely returning a pair of glasses Ms. Simpson had left in a restaurant. Ms. Simpson's throat was cut so completely she was nearly decapitated.

Police later found evidence at O.J. Simpson's **Brentwood mansion** that they used to charge the football star with the murders. In addition to a history of spousal battery, at the time of the murders Simpson was working on a movie about Navy SEALs, where he'd learned commando-knife techniques. With the entire world watching from news helicopters, police arrested Simpson at his house at the conclusion of a notorious daylong slow-speed car chase around Southern California.

After a yearlong televised trial, Simpson was acquitted of the criminal charges.

Undeterred by the verdict, the Goldman and Brown families sued Simpson in a wrongful death civil suit and won a $33.5 million judgment. Simpson continues to claim that he is penniless not to mention innocent. He was forced to sell his house and other personal items at auction, including his Heisman trophy.

THE SCENES:

Nicole Brown Simpson's Condo
875 South Bundy Drive
Los Angeles, CA

O.J. Simpson's House
360 North Rockingham (at Ashford)
Brentwood, CA
The house was sold in 1997 and torn down in 1998.

WHODUNIT HOTEL

Solvang's Danish Country Inn Bed & Breakfast
818-785-7700
310-836-7700
murder1@murdermystery.com
www.murdermystery.com/weekends

Guests at Solvang's Danish Country Inn Bed & Breakfast witness murders on Saturday and solve them on Sunday.

Colorado

Rocky Mountain High has some serious criminal lows.

Statewide, Colorado is extremely hot for its favorite son, Alferd Packer, the wagon train guide whose indelible contribution to "road food" has been celebrated in song, stage, and crime scenes around the state ever since Packer ate his snowbound clients at Donner Pass.

So, crime scene fans, in the words of Mr. Packer, bon appetit! There's plenty for everybody. Let's chow down on Colorado.

The Nation's Only Ultra Maximum-Security Prison

United States "SuperMax" Penitentiary
5880 State Highway 67
Florence, CO 81226
719-784-9454

Just a few miles southeast of the old territorial prison in Cañon City, the who's who of mass-murdering bombers play house in the nation's only ultra high-tech, ultra maximum-security prison, known as "SuperMax." It's where the criminal elite meet—for life.

Ted Kaczynski (the Unabomber), the Oklahoma City bomber Timothy McVeigh, and World Trade Center bomber Ramzi Yousef share a prison unit here.

BOULDER

THE STORY: *"Child Beauty Queen Murdered, Pandemonium Reigns"*—1996

It was an American tragedy for the Internet age—the Lindbergh kidnapping meets Geraldo.

On December 25, 1996, in the upscale Chautauqua section of Boulder, a six-year-old beauty queen, JonBenet Ramsey, was missing and a ransom note was found. Despite a thorough search of the home, the little girl's body wasn't found in the basement of her palatial home until after the crime scene had been thoroughly trampled. Evidence showed that the kindergartner was sexually molested, bludgeoned, and strangled. Ratings-hungry reporters and talking-head pundits descended on the site like fleas. Through the magic of satellite uplinks, it was "Film At Eleven!" everywhere, all the time.

When police brought in more crime scene technicians, the Ramseys refused to talk to the police. Instead, they airlifted in attorneys, private investigators, handwriting analysts, public-relations consultants, and a Washington-based "crisis management" firm, in addition to launching a web site. Book and TV-movie deals were being tossed around like snowballs.

In a fairly tragic comedy of errors, with all the conflicting reports and finger-pointing, the story about the handling of the investigation has replaced the actual crime as the real story.

In a historical twist, in the summer of 1998, Boulder parks employees found a note in a plastic bag, weighted with rocks, and holes punched into the ground around the grave of famed Old West killer Tom Horn (see Cheyenne, WY), who's buried with his brother's family in Boulder, Colorado's **Columbia Cemetery**. The typed note read, "Tom Horn killed a 14-year-old boy in Wyoming and was hanged in 1903. If you arrest the Ramseys, we'll leave Tom Horn rest in peace," and it was signed, "Western Just Us."

At press time, no arrests have been made—in any of these cases.

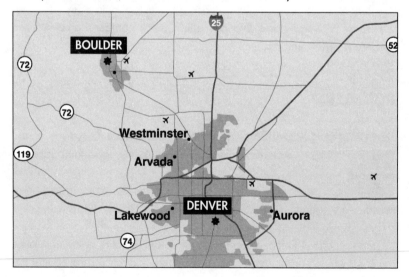

THE SCENES:

The Ramseys' House
755 15th Street
Boulder, CO

Tom Horn's Grave
Columbia Cemetery
Southwest corner of Section C, Lot 74
9th Street, between Pleasant Street
    and College Avenue
Boulder, CO

WHODUNIT HOTEL

Bears Inn Bed & Breakfast
27425 Spruce Lane
Evergreen, CO 80439
800-863-1205
303-670-1205
www.murderattheinn.com

Custom mysteries for groups of eight or more; scheduled weekends for others.

DENVER

THE STORY: *"White Supremacists Gun Down Talk-show Host"—1984*

 After being insulted repeatedly on Alan Berg's **KOA Radio** talk show, members of The Order, a white supremacist hate group, stalked Berg and gunned him down in his driveway as he stepped out of his Volkswagen Beetle. He was struck by thirteen .45-caliber bullets before the suppressed gun jammed. The killers considered the number of bullets fired a sign from God.

Berg's assassination was to be the kick-off for a domestic terror campaign that would rally other white supremacists. The Order went on to steal $4 million in a string of bank and armored car robberies in Northern California. Their trademark was daylight robberies using armor-piercing automatic weapons. The crimes only galvanized law enforcement agencies that spent the summer arresting group members or killing them in shootouts. The money was never recovered.

Sadly, Alan Berg's murder did inspire Timothy McVeigh (see Oklahoma City, Oklahoma), years later, who told buddy Michael Fortier he was headed to Colorado to join an underground racist group like The Order.

The Berg murder was the basis for Eric Bogosian's hit play and movie, *Talk Radio*.

THE SCENE:

Alan Berg Murder Site
1400 Block of Adams (middle of the
   block, between Colfax and 14th
   on east side; garages are at
   street level, the condos above)
Denver, CO

KOA Radio
1380 Lawrence Street
Denver, CO
303-893-8500

LAKE CITY

THE STORY: *"Alferd Packer—Before There Was Trail Mix . . . "—1874*

 In November 1873, despite warnings, Alferd Packer was hired to lead five men to the gold fields near Breckenridge, Colorado. Months later, Packer was the only one to return—looking suspiciously hale and hearty for the survivor of such an ordeal.

At first, he claimed he'd become separated from his clients in a blinding snowstorm and subsisted on rabbits and rosebuds. Later, Packer admitted to eating four of the victims, whom he said died of exposure.

Unfortunately for Packer, the skeletons were discovered at a single campsite at **Donner Pass**, not strung out along the trail as he had claimed. He then explained that he went to scout out a trail and returned to find four men dead from hatchet wounds and Shannon Bell, the fifth man, boiling the flesh of one of the bodies. Bell charged and Packer was forced to defend himself. Days later, Packer had to resort to cannibalism to stay alive.

The charges were reduced to manslaughter and Packer was sentenced to forty years. He spent only five years in prison, however, when he was paroled after a spirited campaign by the *Denver Post* and reporter Polly Pry, who were convinced of his innocence.

An all-star forensic team study in 1989 confirmed many of the details from Packer's second story, enough to establish reasonable doubt in a modern court of law.

Packer's dying words, according to the *Littleton Independent*, the local paper, were "I'm not guilty of the charge."

THE SCENE:

The Alferd Packer Massacre Site (Donner Pass)
South of Alpine Miniature Golf
630 Gunnison Avenue
Lake City, CO 81235

Just five minutes south of the Alpine miniature golf course, you can't miss the sign: two mountain men with an axe driven into their skulls. Once there, look for the plaque, the rock commemorating the site, and five tiny white crosses in honor of Packer's entrées.

TOMB IT MAY CONCERN

Alferd Packer's grave, complete with its original, tiny tombstone.
Littleton Cemetery
Section 3, Lot 65, Grave #8
6155 South Prince
Littleton, CO

Connecticut

Life is deceptively peaceful here in the Constitution State.

One wanted criminal was lulled into such a complete—but false—sense of security he applied for and got a job as a state police dispatcher. He started his first day on the job by entering his name and birthdate into the computer. The system immediately matched it with an outstanding warrant for passing bad checks and he was arrested on the spot.

It's probably no coincidence that Dr. Henry Lee, a star defense witness at the O.J. Simpson trial, is the head of the state's crime lab. He's a very busy man.

DARIEN

THE STORY: *"Globetrotting Rapist 'Vacations' in Europe for Eight Years Before Being Caught"*—1995

Alex Kelly was an 18-year-old wrestling star when he graduated from high school to rape. In February 1986, he was charged with raping two teenage girls four days apart. He pleaded innocent in both cases. Rather than wait around for the trial, Kelly spent the next eight years living the life of a wealthy, suburban Connecticut fugitive: skiing, mountain climbing, and hiding in plain sight with the fast crowd in Europe before he finally surrendered in Switzerland in 1995.

He pleaded no contest to one count of first-degree sexual assault and guilty to a charge of failure to appear for fleeing the country, and no contest to reduced charges in his second rape case. No time was added to his 16-year sentence.

No doubt he is finding the language, skiing, and mountain climbing skills he learned abroad extremely useful in the **MacDougall Correctional Institution** where he will reside until 2013.

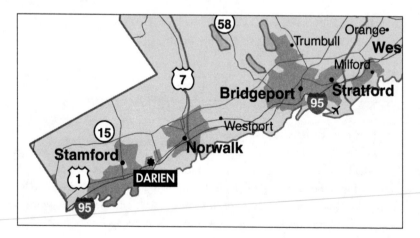

MacDougall Correctional Institution
1153 East Street South
Suffield, CT
860-627-2100

Delaware

Delaware may be the First State in the union. But when it comes to crime scenes, it's a lot closer to the last state in the union.

As a result, the criminal minds are fairly unsophisticated.

In 1999, a bank robber in Wilmington ran off with the loot. Just as he disappeared, a dye packet concealed in the stack of bills exploded, staining his skin fluorescent orange. As police cars cruised the area, a man stepped out of an apartment building and gave a big, friendly wave to the officers. Within seconds of noticing that the jolly good fellow had fluorescent orange hands, he was taken into custody.

"If he would have gone about his business," a police spokesman admitted, "the cop car would have gone right past him."

WILMINGTON

THE STORY: *"Governor's Assistant Murdered by Lover"—1996*

 It was a real-life *Presumed Innocent*, where a powerful prosecutor is accused of killing his mistress. Set in Wilmington, this story starred attorney Thomas Capano, 49, the oldest son of a powerful, wealthy family, and he was convicted and sentenced to die for the crime.

On June 29, 1996, family members began to worry about Anne Marie Fahey. She hadn't been heard from in two days, which was extremely uncharacteristic for her. As the scheduling secretary for state Governor Thomas Carper, she was precise about her commitments.

In her diary, the family found evidence of a long-running affair with Capano, a wealthy, prominent attorney and state power broker who was 17 years her senior. Capano was also the married father of four young daughters.

When questioned by police, Capano admitted the affair but said it had ended six months earlier. With his brothers providing his alibi, the case dragged on for months. Despite the family's intense search efforts, they never found a trace of her.

Meanwhile, police had developed significant circumstantial evidence linking Capano to the crime. After Anne Marie disappeared, he went on a redecorating spree that included a new rug and new chairs to replace the sofa. He also told his housekeeper not to come in on her usual day. Police found a broken fireplace poker, a small axe, and blood droplets on a radiator, a baseboard, and a laundry room door. They also found bottles of blood-stain remover.

The dam broke when Capano's youngest brother, Gerry, came forward and told how, on June 28, 1996, the day before Anne Marie's family began to worry, he'd helped Thomas carry a large white cooler fastened with a chain and a padlock onto Gerry's boat, *Summer Wind*, and tried to sink the cooler 60–70 miles offshore.

But the cooler floated. Gerry shot it with a gun he had on board and saw blood trickle from the hole. It still refused to sink. He then pulled the boat alongside the cooler, handed his brother a spare anchor and walked to the front of the boat and looked away. He didn't want to know what was inside the cooler.

Gerry heard his brother vomiting as he wrestled with the contents of the cooler. As he turned around, he glimpsed a part of a calf and a foot as it disappeared under the water. They broke the lid off the cooler and threw the pieces into the ocean.

Back at his brother's house, he helped him remove the bloodstained rug and furniture and dump the materials in a Dumpster at a construction site owned by another brother. He also had the *Summer Wind* power-cleaned.

The cooler, with a bullet hole in it, was recovered and identified as the one Capano purchased with a credit card from a Wilmington store.

Anne Marie's body was never found.

At the 1998 trial, the prosecution's reconstruction of the murder painted

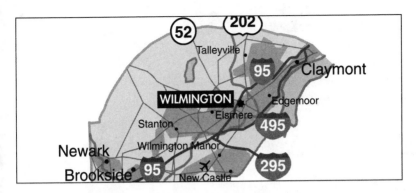

Capano as an obsessive control freak with multiple mistresses who deliberately planned Anne Marie's murder after she broke off their relationship.

After two years of silence about the case, Capano shocked people by admitting that he had dumped Anne Marie's body into the ocean, but he did it to protect another mistress who killed Anne Marie in a jealous rage. The mistress denied Capano's charge.

Capano was convicted directly and the jury overwhelmingly recommended the death penalty.

THE SCENE:

Thomas Capano's House
222 Delaware Ave
Wilmington, DE 19801

Florida

Grifters have been selling Florida "real estate" (a.k.a. swampland) since 1513, when Juan Ponce de León arrived to take possession of the Fountain of Youth. And crime has been flourishing in the state ever since.

In Florida, dead people vote, police chiefs have resigned after allegations of sleeping with inmates' wives, and a U.S. Attorney's career ended after a stripper claimed that he bit her.

Crime scene aficionados, welcome to the Sunshine State.

41

Old Jail
167 San Marco Avenue
Saint Augustine, FL 32084
904-829-3800

The oldest jail in the oldest city in the United States. They've been around since crime was new in this country. You've got to see it.

MIAMI

THE STORY: *"Murph the Surf Pulls Off Crime of the Century"—1964*

 Jack Roland Murphy is the real-life guy that moviemakers base their handsome, athletic, international playboy jewel thieves on. Known as "Murph the Surf" after winning a national surfing championship in the 1950s, Murphy also played violin with the Pittsburgh Symphony and was a tennis star in college.

In addition to stealing over $40,000 in jewels from Eva Gabor when she stayed at **Miami's Racquet Club** in the early 1960s, Murphy became a celebrity thief after he and his gang of beach boys stole the legendary 563-carat Star of India sapphire and the 100-carat Delong ruby from the American Museum of Natural History in New York City. Murphy and the gang were soon caught and convicted. The jewels remained hidden until one of the gang tipped police to their whereabouts, angling for a lighter sentence that he didn't get.

The priceless jewels were stashed in a 25¢-a-day locker at the **old Greyhound Bus Station** in downtown Miami. Murphy's debonair image lost its luster a few years later when he received a life sentence for the 1967 murders of two secretaries whose beaten and garroted bodies were found dumped in Whiskey Creek, a tidal waterway between Miami and Fort Lauderdale.

In 1984, Murphy began a work-release program that allowed him to preach, with the stipulation that he never again set foot in Dade or Broward counties—home of his crime life. The release was later upgraded to a parole. Murphy now has a prison ministry in Dunn, North Carolina, and tours the nation's prisons spreading the gospel.

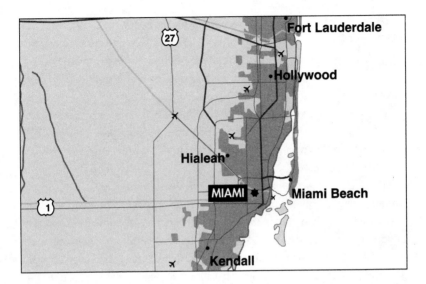

THE SCENES:

The old Greyhound Bus Station
Northwest corner at Northeast First Street and Third Avenue
Miami, FL

The Racquet Club
79th Street Causeway
Miami Beach, FL

Calling All Cars! Museum Alert!

The American Police Hall of Fame & Museum
3801 Biscayne Boulevard
Miami, FL 33137
305-573-0070
policeinfo@aphf.org

Among the 10,000 items in the collection: Harrison Ford's car from *Blade Runner*, an electric chair, gas chamber, guillotine, stocks & pillory, a tramp chair (where vagrants were strapped in and put on public display) and more. The building is easy to find: it has an actual police cruiser hung on the outside.

THE STORY: *"National Murder Spree Ends in Miami Beach"—1997*

 Gay gigolo Andrew Phillip Cunanan was the escort of older wealthy men who bankrolled his expensive lifestyle. Friends say Cunanan's appeal was based on his preppy polish and reckless approach to S&M.

After suddenly finding himself at the opposite end of the social spectrum, Cunanan, destitute and alone, began a murder spree on April 27, 1997, that left bodies of lovers and strangers who got in his way in Minneapolis, Chicago, New Jersey, and Miami Beach. For the next two months, Cunanan was the focus of a nationwide manhunt.

There were Cunanan sightings coast to coast, border to border, including one in a Miami Beach sub shop where a sharp-eyed cashier recognized Cunanan and went into the back to call police. He told his notorious customer he was going for more ingredients. Unfortunately, another cashier, who didn't recognize the most wanted man in America, handed over the sandwich and Cunanan disappeared moments before police arrived.

Cunanan stayed in the rundown **Normandy Plaza Hotel** for two months while the nation searched for him before he came up with a plan.

The culmination of Cunanan's murderous rampage came when he killed internationally renowned clothing designer Gianni Versace. On July 14, 1997, he followed Versace as he walked home from his morning coffee at the nearby **News Café**. As Versace opened the wrought iron gates to his mansion, Cunanan walked up behind him and fired two .40-caliber rounds into the back of his head and fled.

After an intensive search of South Florida, Cunanan was found July 25 in a **houseboat** forty blocks from Versace's murder scene. He'd shot himself in the mouth with the same pistol he'd used on all of his victims.

Andrew Cunanan is buried in San Diego (see California).

THE SCENES:

Gianni Versace Murder Scene
Casa Casuarina
1116 Ocean Drive
Miami Beach, FL

Normandy Plaza Hotel
Rooms 205 and 322
6979 Collins Avenue
Miami Beach, FL
305-866-2500

News Café
2901 Florida Avenue
Miami Beach, FL
305-445-0663

Cunanan's houseboat mooring
5701 Collins Avenue
Miami Beach, FL

TALLAHASSEE

THE STORY: *"Sorority Girls Raped and Murdered While They Slept!"—1978*

It was the final act of a six-state murder spree. After escaping from a Colorado jail, Ted Bundy settled into a Tallahassee boarding house down the street from Florida State University and promptly began stalking co-eds—especially pretty, dark-haired cheerleader-types who parted their hair down the middle.

After spending several nights at the **Silver Dollar Saloon** chatting up sisters from the **Chi Omega sorority house** next door, Bundy broke into the sorority house on January 15, 1978, and attacked four women as they slept. Lisa Levy and Margaret Bowman had been beaten to death with an oak limb, while two other sisters were severely injured. Levy and Bowman also had bite marks, which investigators later matched to Bundy's teeth and used in court to help convict him. Levy was also sexually assaulted.

On February 9, 1978, 12-year-old Kimberly Diane Leach was abducted from outside her school in Lake City, Florida. Her brutalized body was found in a pig trough a few days later.

Bundy's killing spree ended on February 15, 1978, when he was arrested in Pensacola after scuffling with a patrolman. While he was in jail, murder charges from the rest of the United States, and his modus operandi, caught up to him and police began linking Bundy to gruesome unsolved crimes. He was convicted of the Tallahassee and Lake City murders and sentenced to die in Florida's electric chair.

Eleven years later, Bundy was electrocuted by the state of Florida at 7:16 A.M. on January 24, 1989. While waiting for his appeals, he married and fathered a child.

The Chi Omega sorority house was completely remodeled after the killings. The downstairs rooms where the sorority sisters were killed are now used for storage because no one wants to sleep in them. The Silver Dollar Saloon has been razed and replaced by a private dormitory complex.

THE SCENES:

Chi Omega Sorority House
661 West Jefferson
Tallahassee, FL

Ted Bundy's Boarding House
401 West College Avenue
Tallahassee, FL

Silver Dollar Saloon Site
(now Southgate Residence Hall)
675 West Jefferson
Tallahassee, FL

Georgia

With serial killers, lust murders, and more, there's plenty here to keep Georgia on your minds for a long time, crime scene fans.

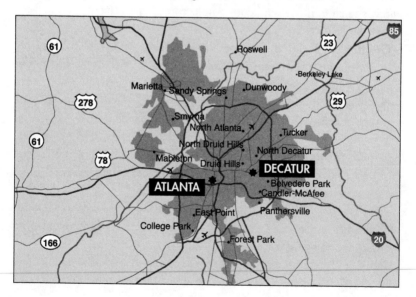

ATLANTA

THE STORY: *"Child Killer Stalks Atlanta! 30-Plus Children Murdered"—1979*

Someone was killing African-American children and teens in Atlanta. At least 24 were murdered in the 22-month period when the investigation formally began on July 28, 1979, before a suspect, Wayne Bertram Williams, was apprehended and tried.

In May 1981, after hearing a splash before dawn, police posted on the **Chattahoochee River Bridge** stopped Williams, 23, and found a nylon rope, gloves, and a bloodstain on the front seat of his car. The stain was later matched to two of the victims. Fiber evidence from Williams' German shepherd was found on one of the victims.

In 1982, Williams was convicted of murdering two of the oldest victims, 27-year-old Nathaniel Cater and 21-year-old Jimmy Ray Payne but none of the others. He received concurrent life sentences. Atlanta police believe he is responsible for the other murders. As proof, they claim that the child murders stopped with Williams' arrest. However, not all agree on Williams' guilt or that the killings have stopped.

In 1985, two of the homicide detectives who worked on the case told NBC's *Dateline* that they believe Williams is innocent.

THE SCENE:

Chattahoochee River Bridge
James Jackson Parkway and South Cobb Drive
Atlanta, GA

Be On the LookOut (BOLO):
Serial Killer Alert!!!

"Suspected Atlanta Lust Killer": At least 10 black prostitutes have been murdered over the last 15 years. All the bodies were found posed in grotesque positions. As of this writing, no suspects have been arrested.

DECATUR

THE STORY: *"Heiress Kidnapped, Buried Underground"—1968*

 On December 17, 1968, an ill 20-year-old Emory College student, Barbara Jane Mackle, was being cared for by her mother off-campus at the nearby **Rodeway Inn** in Decatur. Barbara's father was a multimillionaire South Florida developer and close friend of President Nixon.

Before dawn, Gary Steven Krist and Ruth Eisemann-Schier forced their way into the room at gunpoint, tied and chloroformed the mother, and took Barbara to **Berkeley Lake**, 20 miles northeast of Atlanta, and buried the heiress in a box that had been fitted with an air pump, food, water laced with sedatives, and a battery-powered lamp that went out before she was rescued by the FBI 83 hours later.

Back in Miami, the kidnappers demanded—and received—a $500,000 ransom. On December 20, they phoned the FBI's Atlanta office and told them where to find Mackle. Krist and Eisemann-Schier were later captured by the FBI and Coast Guard while trying to escape by boat.

While awaiting trial, Krist confessed to several murders in Utah and Alaska in the early 1960s. Convicted of kidnapping on May 26, 1969, he was sentenced to life in prison. Amazingly, he was paroled in 1979.

Krist returned to his native Sitka, Alaska, went to medical school in Mexico and Grenada, and has dropped from sight each time his identity became known. Barbara Jane Mackle returned to Miami and married her fiancé from the time of the kidnapping. She doesn't grant interviews. Eisemann-Schier has dropped from sight.

THE SCENES:

The Rodeway Inn has been torn down, but it was next to the Veterans Administration Hospital.
1670 Claremont Road
Decatur, GA

Barbara Jane Mackle's "Burial" Site
South Berkeley Lake Road, about a mile from City Hall, on the right.
Berkeley Lake, GA

SAVANNAH

THE STORY: *"The Real Murders in the Garden of Good and Evil"—1981*

 On May 2, 1981, bisexual hustler Danny Hansford was shot to death by his employer and part-time lover, Jim Williams, a rich antiques dealer and classic house restorer. Williams claimed self-defense, but the crime scene showed signs of a murder doctored to look like self-defense. Williams was quickly convicted. Then he hired more attorneys and a voodoo priestess who put curses on the prosecuting attorneys. His appeals resulted in new trials. During subsequent re-trials, Williams continued to run his business and write articles for *Architectural Digest* from jail.

Williams became the only person in Georgia history ever tried for the same murder four times. Seven months after finally being acquitted, he died, in January 1990.

The murder and its saga provided John Berendt with all the elements of a best-selling book and movie: the Old South, Savannah's social elite, crimes of passion, flamboyant transvestites, a voodoo priestess, and the city's most beautiful historic homes.

Midnight in the Garden of Good and Evil was one of the longest-running *New York Times* hardcover bestsellers—fiction or nonfiction—of all time with 192 weeks on the list, spawning tremendous media coverage and a 1997 feature film of the same name.

With all the hoopla, it's midnight around the clock here. You can call Savannah Walks to schedule a tour of the important sites associated with the *Midnight* legend.

Savannah Walks
888-SAV-WALK

Call to reserve a spot in the tour, which occurs at 1 P.M. daily, and lasts nearly 2 hours.

THE SCENE:

Danny Hansford Murder Scene
429 Bull Street
Savannah, GA

Hawaii

There's more to paradise than pineapples, surfing, volcanoes, and the hula. Despite what the producers of *Hawaii Five-O* would have you believe, there is real crime in Hawaii. What makes Hawaii a paradise for crime scene fans is that you can visit the sites of real crime and *Hawaii Five-O*.

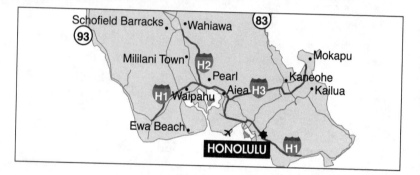

HONOLULU, OAHU

Book 'im, Danno!

As soon as you see the big wave rolling in and hear the trumpets of Morton Stevens' surf-oriented theme, you know crime, usually in the form of the diabolical Wo Fat, is about to be thwarted by the steely-eyed, pompadoured crimefighter Steve McGarrett (played by Jack Lord) and his elite state police squad, known as Five-O. They were so elite, they only reported to the governor.

The longest continuously running police show in the history of television, it ran from September 26, 1968, to April 26, 1980. The Ventures' version of the show's theme went to #4 on Billboard's Top 60 chart in 1969.

The Five-O headquarters was set in the **Iolani Palace**, which now houses a museum. It was originally the residence of King Kalakaua, and later Hawaii's legislature and courts.

McGarrett, a former Navy Commander, was always dispatching his detectives on unbelievably impossible tasks. When something happened in the field, one of the detectives would invariably radio in a report with, "Patch me through to McGarrett."

McGarrett's signature line arrived with the show's conclusion. Just as the evildoer was about to be led off in handcuffs, McGarrett would turn to his top assistant, Danny Williams (played by James MacArthur), and utter a triumphant, "Book 'im, Danno. Murder One."

Iolani Palace (McGarrett's Headquarters)
The corner of South King and Richards Streets in Downtown Honolulu
Informational recording: 808-538-1471
Reservations for tours of the palace: 808-522-0832

The Ilikai Hotel
177 Ala Moana Boulevard
Honolulu, HI

At the end of the opening credits, the camera would rapidly zoom in on Jack Lord standing on the roof of the **Ilikai Hotel**.

THE STORY: *"Cowabungled, Dude!"—1996*

The number one rule of crime: be inconspicuous.

In 1996, while planning to murder his wife, Richard Star went to a **surf shop** and purchased a surfboard bag to dispose of the body. To make sure it was the right size, he insisted on climbing into it in the store, telling the salesperson that he was a movie director and he needed it for a scene where the heroine escapes by hiding in the bag. Once inside the bag, he told the salesperson, "Gee, it sure is spooky in here. I'd hate to have it zipped up." So much for inconspicuous.

When the police found Mrs. Star's body in the floating bag, they knew exactly who to call.

Star is now hanging ten-to-life in a mainland prison.

THE SCENE:

The Town & Country Surf Shop
Ala Moana Shopping Center
1450 Ala Moana Boulevard
Honolulu, HI 96814

Be On the LookOut (BOLO):
Serial Killer Alert!!!

From 1985–1986, the bodies of five women were found in Hawaii. They'd all been bound, manually strangled, and some were raped. Though police are withholding more precise details of the killings, they are convinced that one person is responsible for all five murders.

An FBI profile of the killer describes him as a white man in his late thirties or early forties, driving a light-colored cargo van.

Hawaii's first—and, thus far, only—serial murder case remains unsolved. The killer is still at large.

THE STORY: *"Murder on a Pacific Atoll"—1974*

 Described as "a postcard paradise with a dangerous heart," **Palmyra Atoll, 1,000 miles south of Hawaii**, has been immersed in tales of murder and buried treasure since the days of Spanish galleons. This story was told in the 1991 Vincent Bugliosi bestseller *And the Sea Will Tell* and later that year in a TV-movie with the same name. Bugliosi represented the defendants at the trial.

Eleanor and Malcolm Graham were on an around-the-world sail in 1974 when they were captivated by the atoll's isolated, lush beauty. They liked it so much they anchored their boat, *The Sea Wind*, there for several months. They were never seen alive again.

According to radio broadcasts Malcolm made to a friend, a young couple had sailed into their secluded inlet and tried to befriend them. Several months later, Buck Walker and Stephanie Stearns sailed into Hawaii with the Grahams' boat and a story about how the Grahams disappeared when their inflatable dinghy overturned in the island's surf.

In 1981, a South African couple found Eleanor's skull and some of her jewelry washed up on the shore of Palmyra, along with a metal box. The subsequent investigation determined that she'd been shot to death and the metal box had contained human remains.

Walker and Stearns were captured at the **Hawaii Yacht Club**, still living on the Grahams' boat.

Buck Walker was convicted of Eleanor Graham's murder and is serving a life sentence. Stephanie Stearns, defended by Vincent Bugliosi, the L.A. prosecutor who put Charles Manson away, was acquitted.

Malcolm Graham's body has never been found.

THE SCENE:

Hawaii Yacht Club
1739-C Ala Moana Boulevard
Honolulu, HI

Idaho

Crime is more than small potatoes in the Gem State. They've got big-league bank robbers, political assassins, and an old-time penitentiary to store them in.

Crime scene fans, this spud's for you.

CALDWELL

THE STORY: *"Ex-Governor Blown Up by Assassins in Labor War"—1905*

 On a peaceful December 30 in 1905, former Governor Frank Steunenberg was walking home from his office for dinner. He waved to his young daughter who'd been watching for him from her downstairs bedroom window. He didn't see the tripwire as he closed the front gate to his house and set off an explosion that shredded his legs. Steunenberg died, conscious to the last, on his daughter's bed two hours later.

After a massive manhunt, union labor assassin Harry Orchard was quickly captured. He implicated the union's radical leader, William "Big

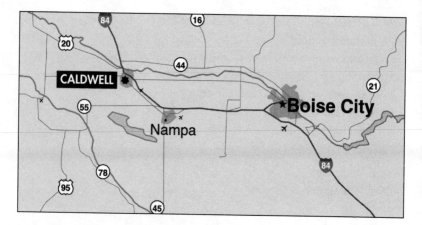

Bill" Haywood, and two others, beginning the very first Trial of the Century in the summer of 1907.

According to Orchard, Haywood wanted to make an example of Steunenberg, who'd campaigned as the "Brother of the Working Man" but declared martial law in Cour d'Alene to control striking miners.

The case set the standard for future Trials of the Century: suspects were kidnapped to stand trial, the confessed killer testified against his bosses, the prosecution was paid for by mining concerns, rampant witness and jury tampering—by the prosecution and the defense—spies in both legal teams, and more.

The cast of characters included: bomber and star witness, union assassin Harry Orchard; legendary defense attorney Clarence Darrow; master Pinkerton detective James McParland (who, in post-Civil War coalfields of Pennsylvania, infiltrated a group of radical bombers known as the Molly Maguires and brought all 30 of them to justice); prosecutor William E. Borah, who served in the U.S. Senate until 1940; President Theodore Roosevelt; his successor, William Howard Taft; and more.

It even had the turn-of-the-century equivalent of Camp O.J., as big-city reporters telegraphed their stories to their editors. It was a national sensation.

Following Darrow's famous 11-hour-and-15-minute summation, the defendants were acquitted.

Harry Orchard was convicted of murder, but in return for his testimony, he was granted clemency, and his sentence was commuted to life in prison. He spent the rest of his time in the Idaho penitentiary as a trusty. When offered parole, Orchard declined and lived out his days in a little house outside the penitentiary where he raised chickens and strawberries.

THE SCENE:
Frank Steunenberg's House
The Steunenberg house burned down in 1913. There are now three lots sharing the space at the southeast corner of Dearborn and 16th. The Caldwell Public Library has a photo of Steunenberg's house and maps for a walking tour of town.
Caldwell, ID

MONTPELIER

THE STORY: *"Butch Cassidy and the Sundance Kid Rob Bank"—1896*

The paper called it "a regular Kansas holdup." On August 13, 1896, two men rode up to the bank, invited the tellers who were out in front having a smoke to join them inside, then proceeded to rob the bank and ride calmly out of town without firing a shot or causing a fuss—a classic Butch Cassidy (a.k.a. Robert Leroy Parker) bank job. The robbery was so smooth and uneventful, they didn't know it was a Butch Cassidy job until Bob Meeks, a known associate of Cassidy's, was identified *years* later.

Every year or so, the Chamber of Commerce stages a reenactment of the robbery. Call for dates.

THE SCENES:

Montpelier Bank Building (now Mountain Litho.)
Check out the sign across the street for more history.
833 Washington Street
Montpelier, ID 83254

Butch Cassidy Bank Robbery Reenactment
Dates vary. Call the Bear Lake Valley Regional Commission.
800-448-BEAR

Old Idaho Penitentiary
2445 Old Penitentiary Road
Boise, ID 83712
208-334-2844

From 1870–1974, if you did the crime in Idaho, you did the time here. Built by convicts to hold convicts (they even quarried the stone from nearby hills), the prison survived five riots and over 500 escapes and escape attempts. Approximately 90 inmates are still "at large."

It has the "most informative prison tour in the West—aside from Alcatraz," according to state guidebooks. You'll see the punishment block, known as "Siberia," Death Row, the gallows area, and the prison's (striped) shirt factory. The museum has a real ball and chain and an "Oregon Boot," a metal device that locked a prisoner's foot and ankle to prevent running.

Illinois

Welcome to the Heartland.

According to the Associated Press, in 1998, for the first time ever, Chicago was the nation's murder capital, surpassing perennial champ New York City, despite a 10-year low in murders and a stringent anti-handgun policy. On a per capita basis, Chicago's 1998 homicide rate is more than double that of New York.

Chicago is so proud of its notorious past that buildings with gangster-era bullet holes in them are regularly preserved. One fellow from Canada purchased the brick wall that St. Valentine's Day Massacre victims were lined up against.

Suffice it to say that when it comes to crime scenes, the Prairie State doesn't have a "prairie" of going by unnoticed.

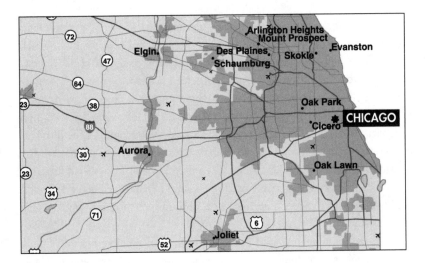

CHICAGO

THE STORY: *"A Night of Horror: Drifter Rapes, Tortures, Murders Eight Student Nurses"—1966*

By the time he'd reached his mid-twenties, Richard Franklin Speck had accumulated 37 arrests for crimes like public drunkenness, disorderly conduct, and burglary. Before the massacre that he became notorious for—eight victims in one night—Speck was suspected of murdering a dozen others in a three-month period in 1966. But frequent trips out on the lake kept him ahead of investigators.

On July 13, Speck forced his way into **Jeffrey Manor**, a two-story townhouse occupied by student nurses from nearby **South Chicago Community Hospital**. The townhouse was a half-block from the union hall.

As he rounded up the nurses and tied them up, he told them he only wanted their money for a trip to New Orleans. Several more nurses arrived after Speck had taken over the house. They were quickly tied up with all the others.

Unfortunately, the students only had a miniscule amount of money. One by one, Speck led eight terrified women, all in their early twenties, to other rooms where he alternately strangled, raped, sodomized, or tortured them to death.

While Speck was out with each consecutive victim, the remaining women desperately tried to hide under the bed. But it was a futile effort. It wasn't until the end of the slaughter that Speck lost count of his victims. Only Corazon Amurao managed to remain hidden. She made her way to the balcony and called down for help after Speck had finally gone.

Speck wasn't on the loose for long. From the use of square knots to bind the victims, police suspected they were looking for a seaman. They also had Amurao's recollection of Speck's desire to travel to New Orleans and her description of a prominent tattoo, "Born to Raise Hell," on his left forearm.

While Speck was in the hospital on July 17 after a bungled suicide attempt, doctors recognized the tattoo and the police quickly took Speck into custody.

One month after his April 1967 conviction for multiple murder, Speck was sentenced to death. However, while he awaited appeal, the U.S. Supreme Court ruled capital punishment unconstitutional and overturned his sentence. Speck was resentenced to consecutive life terms totaling more than 400 years. He died of natural causes in prison in December 1991.

THE SCENES:

Jeffrey Manor
2319 East 100th Street
Chicago, IL

South Chicago Community Hospital (now Trinity Hospital)
2320 East 93rd Street
Chicago, IL

There is a small memorial garden near the administrative part of the hospital to honor the memory of the nurses Speck murdered. The nursing school will be putting up a plaque soon.

* * * * * *

THE STORY: *"Last Show for Public Enemy Number One"*—1934

 The nationwide manhunt for America's most wanted criminal, John Dillinger, came to a bloody end out-side the **Biograph Theater** on July 22, 1934. Despite the number of people he'd gunned down, Dillinger had captured the public's imagination as the latest Robin Hood, robbing from the rich banks and distributing some of the proceeds to the Depression-era poor.

Pressured by police, local madam Anna Sage, known as "The Lady in Red" for the highly visible outfit she wore on the night of the shootout, told legendary FBI agent Melvin Purvis that she and a girlfriend would be going to see *Manhattan Melodrama* with Dillinger that evening.

As the Dillinger party exited the theater, Purvis struck a match and lit a cigar to signal the other agents to move in. A moment later, Dillinger, sensing the trap, crouched and ran into a nearby alley and a shootout ensued. Dillinger's bullet-ridden body fell across the sidewalk in front of the alley.

Anna Sage was later deported to Rumania, where she died of liver disease in 1947. Purvis shot himself in 1960 with the Colt .45 pistol his fellow agents gave him to commemorate Dillinger's capture. The Biograph Theater is still operating today.

THE SCENE:

Biograph Theater
2433 Lincoln Avenue
Chicago, IL
773-348-4123

Scarface Lived Here

Capone's Chicago House
7244 South Prairie Avenue
Chicago, IL

Al Capone, Chicago's best known criminal, moved to Chicago from New York in 1919 and ran organized crime in the city from 1924 until 1931, when he was jailed for tax evasion. His wife, Mae, son, "Sonny," and other relatives lived here, while Al preferred to live in the city and stay closer to the action.

AL CAPONE—
BIG AL HIMSELF.

THE STORY: *"Seven Gangsters Slaughtered on St. Valentine's Day"—1929*

 The most notorious event in Chicago gang days was the St. Valentine's Day Massacre.

At about 10:30 A.M. four men burst into the **S.M.C. Cartage Co. garage,** a warehouse for Capone rival George "Bugs" Moran's bootlegging enterprise.

The first two to enter were dressed as policemen, and they ordered the seven men in the garage—six Moran associates and Reinhardt Schwimmer, an optometrist and gangster groupie—to line up against a whitewashed brick wall.

The gunmen sprayed the wall with their Thompson submachine guns, filling the seven men with over 100 bullets.

No one was ever tried for the crime.

Amazingly, Frank Gusenberg, a top Moran aide and hardcore criminal to the end, was still alive when police arrived, despite having fourteen bullets lodged in his body. He lived for three hours after the shooting and refused to tell the police anything.

The old garage was demolished in 1967, right after it was used as a location for the movie *The St. Valentine's Day Massacre* starring Jason Robards and George Segal.

The site now houses a senior center. To this day, people walking past report hearing screams and machine-gun fire, and that animals are particularly bothered by the place, sometimes barking, howling, and whining in fear.

THE SCENE:

S.M.C. Cartage Co. Garage Site
2122 North Clark Street
Chicago, IL

Read more about the site at www.prairieghosts.com/valentine.html

Al Capone's Speakeasy and Steak House

(the *de facto* Al Capone museum)
35W 337 Riverside Drive (call for directions)
St. Charles, IL
888-SPEAKEASY
847-741-1244

Have a steak and enjoy the Caponiana in this actual 1920s speakeasy. In the men's room, there is a sign over the urinals attesting to the fact that Big Al "hung out" there.

TOMB IT MAY CONCERN

Al Capone's Tombstone
Mount Carmel Cemetery
1400 South Wolf Road
Hillside, IL 60162
708-449-8300

Capone's body was originally buried at Mt. Olivet Cemetery, but it was moved here after being repeatedly vandalized. The graves of former Capone rivals Deanie O'Bannion and Hymie Weiss are nearby.

Capone is in Section 35. At the main entrance go right approximately six markers and there is a gray marker with a large bush in front of it—hiding the name Capone.

Jack Ruby, the man who murdered Lee Harvey Oswald (see Dallas, Texas) as he was being escorted by police, is also buried here.

* * * * * *

THE STORY: *"Lipstick Killer Begs Police:*
'Catch Me Before I Kill More!'"—1952

 William Heirens' troubled childhood, which included cross-dressing, a Nazi fascination, and an arrest for bringing a loaded pistol to school, officially ended on June 3, 1945, when at age 16 he discovered sexual gratification while burgling a **sleeping woman's apartment. Josephine Ross** woke up and Heirens cut her throat and stabbed her several times. Then he spent the next two hours wandering around the apartment enjoying multiple orgasms. Afterward, even though she was dead, he bandaged her neck.

On December 10, 1945, Heirens broke into the **apartment of 33-year-old Frances Brown**. He shot her twice as she stepped out of the bathroom, before she could scream, then killed her with a knife from her kitchen. He pulled her body into the bathroom to wash the blood away, leaving Brown's body draped across the tub, partially covered with a housecoat.

On the bathroom mirror, using her lipstick, he wrote, "For Heaven's sake catch me before I kill more. I cannot control myself."

A month later, he broke into the **bedroom of six-year-old Suzanne Degnan**, kidnapped her, and left a ransom note demanding $20,000 to misdirect the police. He dragged her to a nearby basement and killed her, dismembering her body with a hunting knife. He wrapped the pieces in paper and dropped them in storm drains on his way home.

Heirens was caught on June 26, 1946, when police answered a prowler call on Chicago's north side. He told police that the murders were committed by another person who'd occupied his body named "George Murman," the surname short for "Murder Man." Heirens' insanity plea was dismissed and he received three consecutive life terms.

In 1946, *Time* magazine considered the case "The Crime Story of the Century." In April 1983, a federal judge considered Heirens rehabilitated and ordered his release. That ruling was overturned on appeal by the prosecution. Heirens remains in prison, but still maintains that "George Murman" is the real culprit.

THE SCENES:

Josephine Ross's House
4108 Kenmore Avenue
Chicago, IL

Suzanne Degnan's House
5943 Kenmore Avenue
Chicago, IL

Frances Brown's House
3941 Pine Grove Avenue
Chicago, IL

Calling All Cars! Museum Alert!

American Police Museum
1717 South State Street
Chicago, IL
312-431-0005
www.policemuseum.com

Have a seat in the replica of the Illinois State Prison electric chair and get a mild buzz when the switch is thrown. You can also take your own mug shot photo.

DES PLAINES

THE STORY: *"Odor Leads Police to 29 Bodies Buried under House"—1978*

 On December 12, 1978, Robert Piest left his job at a Chicago pharmacy and disappeared. He had told friends and family that he was meeting with the contractor who'd recently remodeled the pharmacy, John Wayne Gacy, Jr. When police arrived at Gacy's house to question him, they recognized the odor of decomposing bodies immediately and arrested him. In the crawlspace under the house, police unearthed 29 bodies. Another 4 were found in the nearby river.

Gacy was convicted on all 33 counts at his 1980 murder trial and received life sentences for the 21 murders that occurred before June 21, 1977, when Illinois reinstated capital punishment. He received a death sentence for the remaining 12 murders that occurred after July 1977.

Gacy was executed on May 9, 1994, the anniversary of his first arrest in 1968 for sodomy (see Waterloo, Iowa).

Gacy's chilling final words were found on the back of a painting he'd made on Death Row, "Find the bodies if you can."

THE SCENE:

John Wayne Gacy's House
8213 West Summerdale Avenue
Des Plaines, IL

Indiana

In the Hoosier State, crime *and* basketball are religions, but athletes are still held to moral standards. Although it's sometimes hard to tell.

TOMB IT MAY CONCERN

John Dillinger's Grave
Crown Hill Cemetery
700 West 38th Street
Indianapolis, IN

LA PORTE

THE STORY: *"Lady Bluebeard Kills 14 Lonely Hearts Suitors, Collects Insurance Money"—1908*

After delivering a series of fatal accidents to wealthy men and filing insurance claims, local hog farmer and butcher Belle Gunness was arrested by local police. But before they could arrest her, her farm mysteriously burned down, leaving a headless female corpse, Gunness's dentures, and an abnormally large pile of human bones.

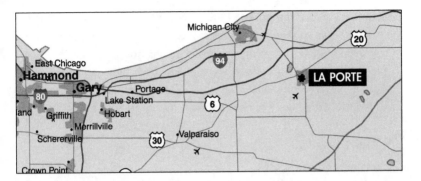

Though police concluded that Gunness had faked her own death, they were unable to capture her.

It is believed that she was last seen in an Ohio bordello in 1935.

Police have evidence of 14 known victims, but they suspect that the real total is closer to 50–100 murders, the remains of which were fed to Gunness's hogs.

THE SCENE:

Belle Gunness Farm
(near Fishtrap Lake)
State Highway 39 South
to the outskirts of La Porte.
La Porte, IN

Crime Factoid: Seymour is the hometown of contemporary outlaw rocker John Mellencamp, who's spurned Hollywood and New York to live in Bloomington, IN.

SEYMOUR

THE STORY: *"Reno Brothers Commit First U.S. Train Robbery"—1866*

In the fall of 1865, brothers Frank, John, Simeon, and William Reno formed a gang that terrorized the Seymour area for the next four years.

On October 6, 1866, John and Simeon Reno and Franklin Sparks boarded an Ohio & Mississippi train as it pulled out of the Seymour depot. After knocking a guard unconscious, they pushed two safes off the train on the outskirts of town where the rest of the gang waited for them.

The robbery netted the gang $15,000 and the honor of committing the first official train robbery in U.S. history, a crime innovation that had originally been credited to the more popular James gang.

Frank, William, and Simeon were pulled from their jail cell by vigilantes in New Albany and hanged on December 12, 1868, as they awaited trial. They were buried together in a large pine box.

THE SCENES:

Reno Family Farm

Drive into Riverview Cemetery (Ewing and 16th Street) and follow the drive to the top of the low hill. Stop when you're facing west. The area across the railroad tracks below is the farm.

Reno Brothers' Grave

There are two cemeteries in Seymour between 9th and 11th streets on Ewing. From the old Seymour City Cemetery, the closest cemetery to 9th and Ewing, follow 9th Street one half-block to the new marker atop a stone pillar on the right. The grave is on the nearby incline, inside the wrought iron fence.

Iowa

The Hawkeye State is a very quiet place, but it's not completely dead. It does have its crime scene charms.

Prisoners Are Shaken, Not Stirred in Rotating Jail

The Squirrel Cage Jail
226 Pearl Street
Council Bluffs, IA 51503
712-323-2509

Law enforcement personnel are always complaining about revolving jails, but this isn't what they mean. A sister to a jail in Crawfordsville, Indiana, this lazy susan for criminals was built in 1885. The cells revolve to give jailers an unobstructed view of all the cells. Use of the jail was discontinued in 1969, after it became a hazard to inmates. Hardened criminals often shattered while tumbling.

WATERLOO

THE STORY: *"John Wayne Gacy's Kentucky Fried Chicken Stand"—1968*

 They've all got to start somewhere. Though John Wayne Gacy, Jr. would go on to achieve complete infamy in Des Plaines, Illinois, he officially started his career as a homosexual abuser, sodomist, and general pervert here. In 1968, at the age of 26, a married man and manager at one of his father-in-law's **fast food stands**, Gacy lured a boy into the back room after closing time, handcuffed him, and tried to pay him to perform oral sex. When that failed, he tried to sodomize the boy. The youth escaped and reported him to police.

Gacy's attempt to have the boy roughed up before the trial failed and he drew a ten-year sentence. However, because he didn't have a criminal record, and he was a model prisoner, Gacy was released after 18 months, and he moved to the Chicago area in 1971.

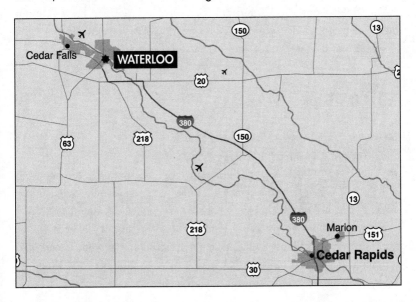

Kansas

Old West crime and contemporary crime come together in Kansas.

Cattle towns like Dodge City, Ellsworth, Hays, and Wichita gave many a Western outlaw and legendary lawman their reputations. Real lawmen like Wyatt Earp, Bat Masterson, Bill Tilghman, and others were just a few who taught at Dodge City U., where Hamilton Bell, the sheriff who followed Bat Masterson, ushered in modern law enforcement. Crime and Dodge City were never the same again.

After thirty years of enforcing the law, Bell's claim to fame was that he never shot anyone or clubbed anyone with his pistol, yet he took more men into custody with warrants than any other Western lawman.

Modern crimes in Kansas are just as remarkable.

HOLCOMB

THE STORY: *"Farm Family Stabbed and Shot in Their Remote Homestead"—1959*

 It was a rural nightmare come true. One morning in November 1959, a farm family was found butchered in their home outside Garden City.

Herbert Clutter, the 48-year-old father, had his throat slit from ear to ear. His body had been dumped in the basement. His wife, Helen, 45, daughter Nancy, 16, and son Kenyon, 15, were tied in chairs while the killers took turns blowing their heads off with a shotgun.

Hardened criminal Dick Hickock had heard about the Clutters and a safe with $10,000 from a cellmate. Upon his release, he set out with another career criminal, Perry Smith, to rob them. On the night of November 15, 1959, the two burst into **the Clutter home** and tied up the frightened family members. Enraged because they could only find about $50 and no safe, Hickock and Smith slaughtered their helpless victims.

A massive dragnet finally caught the two killers in Las Vegas, Nevada, and they promptly began to incriminate each other. At first, Smith denied killing anyone. Then he said of Herbert Clutter, "He was a nice gentleman. I thought so right up to the time I cut his throat."

Hickock and Smith were convicted in March 1960 and hanged on the gallows inside the Kansas State Prison at Lansing on April 14, 1965.

The Clutter family massacre was detailed in Truman Capote's best-selling classic *In Cold Blood,* which was made into a film and later a TV-movie.

THE SCENE:

The Clutters' House
600 Oak Avenue
Holcomb, KS

MEADE

THE STORY: *"Hide With the Dalton Gang!"—1892*

 Eva Dalton and her husband John Whipple were upstanding members of the community—until her outlaw brothers moved into the house she and her husband built. Then they moved out. New owners later found a 95-foot-long tunnel that ran under the house to the barn and gave it a modern crime scene use: it's now the **Dalton Gang Hideout and Giftshop Museum**.

As daring and bold as the contemporary James gang, Eva's brothers constituted the last great bandit gang of the Old West. Part of their legend was based on their Old West chivalry. They refused to rob women on the trains and stagecoaches they held up and they preferred to "die game"

by shooting it out with lawmen rather than be taken alive. It was a point of outlaw honor. Despite their folksy appeal, they were still some of the meanest, most ruthless bandits and killers in the territory. All but Emmett died shooting it out with the law and armed citizens in Coffeyville, Kansas.

Despite absorbing 20 bullets in the disastrous raid on Coffeyville and a long prison sentence, Emmett Dalton spent the last 30 years of his life as a vocal champion of law and order, and became a model citizen happily married to his sweetheart Julia Johnson.

Six years before he died, the last of the Dalton brothers returned to Coffeyville to visit the common grave of his brothers and the other gang members who died in the ill-fated raid. Standing in front of the grave, he pointed to the spot and told the people around him, "I challenge the world to produce the history of any outlaw who ever got anything out of it but that [a grave], or else be huddled in a prison cell . . . The biggest fool on earth is the one who thinks he can beat the law, that crime can be made to pay. It never paid and it never will and that was the one big lesson of the Coffeyville raid."

THE SCENE:

Dalton Gang Hideout and Giftshop Museum
502 South Pearlette Street
Meade, KS 67864
800-354-2743

OLATHE

THE STORY: *"Forger Faxes His Way Out of Jail"*—1999

 In February 1999, Joshua Williams was being held in the **Olathe jail** on forgery charges and probation violation. When police received a fax from the "Govenor" (sic) with the forged signature of an actual parole officer indicating that the charges against Williams would be dropped, they let him go. He was quickly re-arrested. A Kansas Department of Corrections spokesman says they're "real interested in finding the creative mind that faxed that letter."

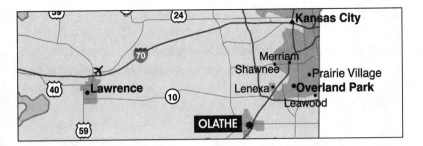

THE SCENE:

Johnson County Adult Detention Center
101 North Kansas Avenue
Olathe, KS
913-791-1100

Be On the LookOut (BOLO): Serial Killer Alert!!!

From 1974–1977, Wichita's "BTK (Bind Torture Kill) Killer" killed six or more people, then called police to brag about the crimes, telling them he wanted to be like David Berkowitz, the "Son of Sam" (see New York, New York). He was so impressed with himself that after tying a young girl to a basement pipe and killing her, he masturbated over her corpse. No suspects have been arrested, even though police have his voice on tape and other trace evidence.

Kentucky

There's more to Kentucky than distilleries (both licensed, such as Jack Daniels, and many more that are unlicensed), the Fort Knox gold reserve, and the Hatfield-McCoy feud.

For example, Jesse James managed to rob a bank there. After visiting the crime scenes here—where else can you spend a night in jail, voluntarily, and get to sleep on a waterbed?—you'll be calling it "My Old Kentucky Home."

RUSSELLVILLE

THE STORY: *"Jesse James Robs Bank!"—1868*

 Still suffering from a Civil War gunshot wound to the lung, Jesse James and the gang hid out at a relative's home in nearby Adairsville. As Jesse regained his strength, he needed money.

At 2:00 P.M. on March 20, Civil War guerillas Jesse and Frank James, Cole and Jim Younger, and George and Oliver Shepherd robbed **Nimrod Long and Company**, a bank in Russellville, at gunpoint after failing to get a very suspicious, large bank note cashed the day before.

One of the robbers shot Mr. Long, the bank manager, but the shot only grazed him, and Long jumped up and raised an alarm as the robbers fled with $9,000 in currency and another $5,000 in coins. Despite a spirited chase by the town's posse, the gang made a successful escape.

Unfazed by the robbery, the bank has been operating continuously since 1839. It moved to a new building down the street and is now called **The Old Southern Bank**. A mural depicting the robbery is painted on the wall in the bank's lobby. The original building is now a private home.

The bank was robbed for the second time on September 22, 1934. The robbers, far more anonymous than the James gang, were never identified.

THE SCENES:

Nimrod Long and Company Robbery Scene
296 South Main Street
Russellville, KY

The Old Southern Bank
Sixth and Main
Russellville, KY

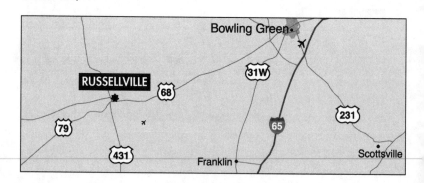

Jesse James Bank Robbery Reenactment
Old Southern Bank Site

Part of the annual Tobacco Festival, the second Saturday in October. Call the Logan County Chamber of Commerce: 502-726-2206.

WHODUNIT HOTELS

Jailer's Inn B&B
111 West Stephen Foster Avenue
Bardstown, Kentucky 40004
800-948-5551
502-348-5551
www.jailersinn.com

It's definitely not the Hyatt. Iron bars guard the windows, while the stone walls are 30 inches thick. A heavy steel door slams behind you like a life sentence.

The building was constructed in 1819, but it has plenty of modern conveniences. The Jail Cell, also known as the "fun room," is the only one that still resembles a cell. It's decorated in black and white. And it now holds two of the original bunks and a waterbed. While being incarcerated here enjoy yourself with a poster of Elvis doing the "Jailhouse Rock" and snuggle up with a James Dean pillow.

Old Talbott Tavern and Inn
107 West Stephen Foster Avenue
Bardstown, Kentucky 40004
800-4-TAVERN
www.talbotts.com

Next door to the jail is the Old Talbott Tavern, the oldest Western stagecoach stop in America. You can eat and sleep in the same rooms as Jesse James, Abraham Lincoln, or Andrew Jackson.

Louisiana

The Pelican State leads the nation in murders per capita (according to the FBI's 1997 crime statistics), which is in sharp contrast to the abundance of antebellum charm and haunted buildings.

So whether your streetcar is named desire, murder, or passion, prepare to be transported.

Crime Scene Calendar Alert!!!

Angola Prison Rodeo
Terrie Leigh Oliveaux Rodeo Arena
Louisiana State Penitentiary
From St. Francisville (the nearest town), go north on Highway 61. Turn left on Highway 66 (Tunica Trace), which leads directly to the front gate of the prison.
Angola, LA
225-655-4411

Every Sunday in October, the inmates ride bulls and broncos, rope calves, and play cards at a table in the middle of the arena while a hostile bull tries to get in the action. The last man to flee wins a prize. One of the most unusual events is Guts & Glory, where inmates try to pluck a chip worth $100 from a bull's forehead.

Hint: go early or you won't get a seat. The only other way to see the rodeo is to commit a felony in Louisiana. But then you don't get to leave after the rodeo's over.

Angola is the alma mater for many of best-selling mystery fiction writer Elmore Leonard's toughest, most notorious villains. The hardcore real-life rapists and murderers who wind up here are much scarier. Eighty percent of the inmates will never leave.

While you're there, check out the prison museum. As the prototypical old-time southern prison, you'll find a ton of fascinating material here. It's to the right of the front door.

GIBSLAND

THE STORY: *"Bonnie & Clyde Shot to Death"—1934*

 Their life together was hardly the stuff of movies. For all the bold robberies and romantic stories written about the lovers, the fact was that it wasn't safe to be between Bonnie Parker and Clyde Champion Barrow and the loot or the exit. The pair, along with various gang members, including Clyde's brother Buck and Buck's wife Blanche, shot their way through numerous robberies, roadblocks, and daring jail-breaks in Texas, Kansas, Missouri, Oklahoma, and Louisiana.

By the time they were gunned down by a posse of federal and local lawmen, the Barrow gang had killed at least thirteen people and wounded twice as many while committing scores of robberies and burglaries. A significant portion of the dead and wounded were police officers.

The yearlong manhunt for Bonnie and Clyde was one of the bloodiest and most spectacular up to that time. Mostly, it was a war of attrition. One by one, the members of the gang died shooting it out with police.

In the end, it was just Bonnie and Clyde in northern Louisiana.

Because the pair seemed unwilling to be taken alive, when a posse finally located the duo before dawn on May 23, 1934, they just started shooting at the car from ambush. Hundreds of rounds later, Bonnie and Clyde had passed on into legend.

THE SCENE:

Bonnie and Clyde Museum
Box 309
Gibsland, LA 71028

The museum is open by appointment only. Write to the address listed above or call Gibsland City Hall at 318-843-6141 between 8 and 5 Monday through Friday to set up a date and time.

The original postcards of their bullet-riddled bodies are highly prized. They never looked like Warren Beatty or Faye Dunaway in *Bonnie & Clyde*—before or after the shootout.

Bonnie and Clyde Murder Site Memorial

A stone marker commemorates the site of the ambush. Go eight miles south of Gibsland along Highway-154. You can't miss it.

Bonnie and Clyde Festival

Gibsland, LA 71028 (about 45 miles east of Shreveport)
Contact Gibsland City Hall for more details.
318-843-6141

An annual celebration is held here to mark the Romeo and Juliet of armed robbery's last visit here—or anywhere. That's when the law ended their crime spree, ventilating them and their automobile near Sailes, Bienville Parish, Louisiana, on May 23, 1934.

The event is always held the weekend in May closest to the 23rd. It's a big Louisiana party with period costumes. Their "air-conditioned" car is on display.

NEW ORLEANS

THE STORY: *"Rampaging Sniper-Arsonist Kills 9, Holds Downtown Hostage from Hotel Rooftop"—1973*

Twenty-three-year-old Mark Essex was an unlikely killer. Authorities still aren't sure what made the soft-spoken African-American former Navy sailor snap and begin hunting white people and police officers. Before police macerated Essex with more than two hundred bullets, the total for his siege was nine dead, ten wounded (including two police officers, an assistant police chief, a honeymooning couple, and two hotel employees). Ten others were injured by shrapnel and stray police bullets.

At 10:15 A.M. on January 7, Essex shot a grocer and hijacked a car, telling the African-American driver that he only wanted to kill "honkies." Police chased Essex into the **Howard Johnson's Hotel**, a block away from City Hall. On his way to the roof, Essex set fire to phone books and placed them under the drapes in several rooms. The fire damaged 44 rooms. In addition, along the way up, at different places in the hotel, he periodically fired a few shots with his .44-magnum carbine rifle and threw lit firecrackers to give the impression of a squad of snipers and arsonists on the loose.

On the roof, he holed up in a concrete service structure and for the next 12 hours held police at bay while shouting, "Power to the people! You'll never take me! Africa! Africa!" For the duration of the siege, police would not know how many people were involved.

After the shootings made the news, armed civilians arrived on the scene and began shooting at Essex. At times, police and citizens were shooting at each other.

Firing from a helicopter, police finally managed to drive Essex from cover. Raising a fist in a power salute, Essex was cut down. Police continued to fire into Essex's body to make sure he was dead, shattering his rifle with the fusillade. Reports of gun flashes and other snipers kept police in battle mode for twelve more hours.

THE SCENE:

Downtown Howard Johnson's Hotel
330 Loyola Avenue
New Orleans, LA
800-446-4656

Be On the LookOut (BOLO):
Serial Killer Alert!!!

The "New Orleans Serial Killer": The bodies of 24 women—mostly prostitutes from Algiers and Treme, two of the poorest neighborhoods of the city—have been winding up in New Orleans, Jefferson Parish, and swamps further west of the city since 1991. A New Orleans police officer was suspected of two of the killings, one of whom was his girlfriend, but charges were never filed.

Maine

There is so little noteworthy crime here, it's hard to believe that master horror writer Stephen King makes it his home.

The closest they have come to a contemporary murder mystery here was in 1998, when officials finally got around to burying the skull of a Bucksport chambermaid whose unsolved murder occurred in 1898. The mystery: trying to figure out how the skull wound up sitting in a courthouse closet for so long.

Still, the Pine Tree State has a sprinkling of worthwhile crime scene cones.

BANGOR

THE STORY: *"Public Enemy #1 Dies in Battle of Bangor"*—1937

Here's further proof that you don't have to be smart to be a criminal, even Public Enemy #1.

Aspiring killer Al Brady's ambition was to "Make Dillinger look like a piker."

By the tender age of 26, Brady had committed four murders and more than 150 robberies. He had been apprehended just once, and followed that with a successful jailbreak.

J. Edgar Hoover said of Brady's gang, "Never in my experience as director of the FBI have I seen a more wanton display of utter conscience-less criminality." Soon Brady reached his goal, becoming Public Enemy #1. With the FBI after him, Brady decided to hole up in Maine, where it was highly unlikely anyone would know him or the gang. So far, so good.

Then, the 26-year-old Brady and his gang, which consisted of Clarence Lee Shaffer, Jr. and James Dalhover, went into Dakin's, the local sporting goods store, to order Thompson submachine guns—the preferred weapon of gunrunners, gangsters, and, oh, notorious killers. Since the store primarily sold deer rifles to local citizens, the owner was a little suspicious when strangers asked to buy automatic weapons. He told the city boys that it would take a week for the weapons to arrive.

To no one's surprise but the Brady gang's, the town was crawling with heavily armed G-men by the time the gang returned. For "camouflage," the gang drove a nondescript Buick luxury sedan with whitewalls to blend in with the weathered trucks driven by the mostly blue-collar locals.

Brady and Schaffer remained in the car while Dalhover went into the store and was promptly arrested. Brady and Schaffer saw their colleague being handcuffed and began shooting.

The G-men returned fire and the Battle of Bangor was on. Sixty seconds and sixty shots later, it was off. Brady and Schaffer had been permanently apprehended (killed). Dalhover was returned to Indiana for trial and electrocuted the following year.

Brady was buried in Bangor's **Mt. Hope Cemetery**.

There is a commemorative plaque marking the site of the gun battle. The manhole covers on the street in front of the plaque are the same ones that Brady died on.

THE SCENES:

Battle of Bangor Crime Scene Plaque
Central Street (at the corner where Main and State meet Central)

Al Brady's Grave
Public Grounds Cemetery
Mt. Hope Cemetery
1038 State Street
Bangor, ME

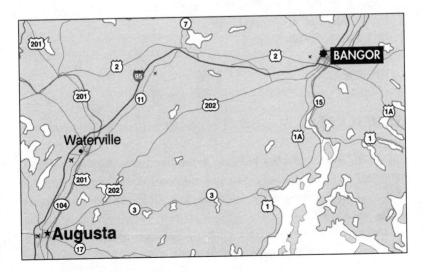

Maryland

Unfortunately for those who commit crimes here, the Free State isn't so lenient when it comes to sentencing, as a first-degree murder carries an automatic life sentence. Notable figures who had their own "life sentence" here include Edgar Allan Poe and John Wilkes Booth.

Calling All Cars! Museum Alert!

The Edgar Allan Poe House and Museum
203 North Amity Street
Baltimore, MD 21223
410-396-7932
Fax: 410-396-5662

Poe penned the classic murder mystery *Murders in the Rue Morgue*. So what if the killer was an orangutan? The story foreshadowed the advent of behavioral profiling techniques that the FBI uses to capture serial killers.

TOMB IT MAY CONCERN

Edgar Allan Poe's Final Resting Place
Westminster Hall & Burying Ground
500 West Baltimore Street
Baltimore, MD
410-706-2072

ST. MICHAELS

THE STORY: *"Murder-Mystery Weekend Turned Live Murder Mystery"—1998*

 A murder-mystery weekend became all too real in the quiet historic town of St. Michaels, just outside Easton, in February of 1998.

Stephen Hricko and his wife Kimberly had been having marital troubles. In an attempt to rekindle the relationship they left their Laurel,

Maryland home and set out on a romantic weekend for Valentine's Day. The hopeful plans couldn't have turned out any worse.

Kimberly said that after Stephen, drunk, attempted to pressure her into sex, she left him to go stay with a friend. Unable to find the friend's house, however, she returned around 1 A.M. Smoke from a fire prevented her from entering the room. She notified the hotel clerk and he and a hotel guest dragged Stephen's badly burned body from the room. Kimberly told police that Stephen often smoked when he drank. Accidental death? Suicide? Not quite.

Because Stephen's family and friends said that he neither smoked nor drank. The autopsy showed not only no alcohol but also no carbon monoxide in his blood. The lack of burns or soot in his trachea and lungs indicated that he had not been breathing during the fire at all. The report suggested poisoning.

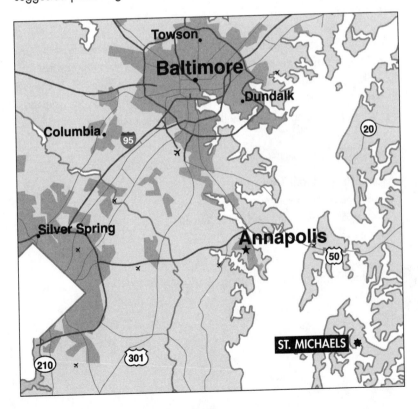

Later, it came out that Kimberly, a surgical technician, had reportedly offered a co-worker $50,000 to arrange her husband's murder a month earlier. To top it all off, she was to collect on her husband's $400,000 life insurance policy.

Though she never admitted guilt, Kimberly Hricko was sentenced to life in prison for murdering her husband, and will concurrently serve a 30-year arson conviction. She plans to appeal.

THE SCENE:

Harbourtowne Golf Resort and Convention Center
Cottage 506
Miles River & Eastern Chesapeake Bay
St. Michaels, Maryland 21663
800-446-9066
410-745-9066

Take MD Route 50 east toward Easton. One mile before Easton, turn right on the Easton Parkway (Route 322). Continue through several traffic lights, turn right onto Route 33 and continue 10 miles on Route 33 through the town of St. Michaels to the entrance of Harbourtowne, past the brick gatehouse, and follow the signs to the resort.

TOMB IT MAY CONCERN

John Wilkes Booth Tombstone
Greenmount Cemetery
Corner of Greenmount and Oliver streets
Baltimore, MD
410-539-0641

Ask for a map to the tombstone. It isn't marked well.

Massachusetts

The crime jewel of New England. Not a state, but a *commonwealth*, Massachusetts has a wealth of uncommon crime scenes to be explored, including the prototypical serial killer (the Boston Strangler), the namesake of the pyramid scheme, record-setting armed robberies, and more.

Murder is such a big part of the Commonwealth's history that Back Bay Brewing Company offers Boston Massacre Lager, Boston Tea Party Porter and Boston Strangler Stout. Surprised by the negative reaction to the Strangler Stout, the brewers have been working on a new name.

You've got to love a place where you can take a college course in murder. Professor Austin Sarat's course, Murder, is even more popular than Human Sexuality. In its first semester, one fifth of the entire student body at Amherst College enrolled in the course.

BOSTON

THE STORY: *"Phantom Strangler Terrorizes City!"*—1962

 From June 14, 1962, to January 4, 1964, the city's women weren't safe from the mysterious Boston Strangler. He entered the most heavily fortified apartments without leaving signs of entry. He sexually molested his victims, strangling them with their bras, stockings, or housecoat cords, and left them naked from the waist down with their legs spread toward the nearest door. Then he'd disappear without a trace.

Six of the victims were between the ages of 55 and 75, with two victims, possibly attributed to the Strangler, aged 85 and 69. The remaining five victims ranged in age from 19 to 23.

Even though Albert DeSalvo, a troubled handyman, made detailed confessions to the crimes, no one has ever been tried for the murders. Authorities currently believe that DeSalvo was probably not the Strangler and that the evidence points to the existence of more than one.

Based on current knowledge of sexual serial killers, who tend to kill the same type of victim, e.g., Ted Bundy liked pretty young women with long

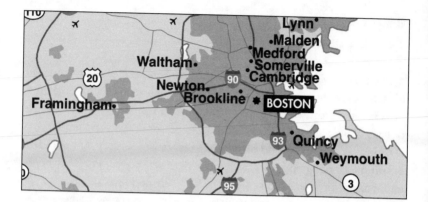

hair parted in the middle, it is now suspected that there was more than one strangler responsible for the murders.

On January 17, 1964, Massachusetts Attorney General Edward Brooke took over the investigation and created a special task force, the Special Division of Crime Research and Detection, more commonly known as "The Strangler Bureau." He selected Assistant Attorney General John S. Bottomly, a controversial choice because of his lack of criminal law experience, to head the division.

Bottomly recruited a team of top-flight investigators and a forensic medical-psychiatric advisory committee. They also hired Dutch psychic Peter Hurkos, who proved to be more trouble than he was worth. Hurkos reportedly posed as an FBI agent once, and led investigators on a wild-goose chase.

Three years earlier, Cambridge police had caught Albert DeSalvo, 29, trying to break into a house. He confessed to being the "Measuring Man," a charming fellow with a clipboard who would call on young women posing as a modeling agent, and ask for their measurements—which they usually let him take with a tape measure—and then leave. The aspiring models began to make police reports after they didn't get called back and discovered that there was no modeling agency.

A pathological braggart, or "a blowhard," in the words of Commissioner McNamara, DeSalvo admitted to breaking into 400 apartments and assaulting some 300 women in a 4-state area. It was hard for police to determine how much of the story was fact or fiction. DeSalvo was committed to Bridgewater State Hospital for observation.

While there, DeSalvo became the confidant of George Nassar, a remorseless killer with a genius IQ and a highly-developed ability to manipulate people. A few months later, DeSalvo confessed to being the Strangler. Nassar referred DeSalvo to his attorney, F. Lee Bailey (see Berkeley, California), who became DeSalvo's new lawyer.

DeSalvo was convicted on previous breaking and entering and assault charges, not the stranglings, and sentenced to life in Walpole State Prison.

In November of 1973, he was stabbed in the heart the night before he was to meet with a psychiatrist and a reporter to reveal who the real Boston Strangler was and why he'd confessed.

In 1968, Tony Curtis and Henry Fonda starred in a feature film about the case, *The Boston Strangler*. Curtis mostly murdered DeSalvo's Boston accent.

Update: In July 1999, the Boston Police Department's Cold Case Squad announced that it was planning to use DNA technology to definitively determine whether Albert DeSalvo was responsible for the killings. However, it won't be easy. Sperm samples from some of the victims and the knife used to kill DeSalvo are missing. Police say they'll exhume DeSalvo's body if they have to.

THE KNOWN, IDENTIFIABLE SCENES:

Anna E. Slesers' House
77 Gainsborough Street
(Back Bay area)
Boston, MA

Nina Nichols' House
1940 Commonwealth Avenue
(Brighton area)
Boston, MA

Ida Irga's House
7 Grove Avenue (West End Area)
Boston, MA

Jane Sullivan's House
435 Columbia Road
(Dorchester area)
Boston, MA

Sophie Clark's House
315 Huntington Avenue
(Back Bay area)
Boston, MA

Patricia Bissette's House
515 Park Drive
(Back Bay area)
Boston, MA

Mary Sullivan's House
44A Charles Street
Boston, MA

Albert DeSalvo's Grave
Puritan Lawn Memorial Park
185 Lake Street
Peabody, MA
978-535-3660

WHODUNIT HOTEL

Lizzie Borden Bed and Breakfast Museum
92 Second Street
Fall River, MA 02721
508-675-7333
lizziebnb@lizzie-borden.com
www.lizzie-borden.com

All together now: Lizzie Borden took an axe / Gave her mother forty whacks / When she saw what she had done / Gave her father forty-one.

The poem commemorates the notorious August 4, 1892, axe murders of banker Andrew Borden and his second wife. Borden's youngest daughter, Lizzie, was charged with the crime and acquitted, but never forgiven.

Now you can spend the night at the murder scene and enjoy the same breakfast the Bordens had on their last day together: bananas, johnny-cakes, sugar cookies, and coffee.

Note: Since the B&B also gives tours to other customers, they aren't kidding when they say checkout is at 10 A.M. They won't axe you twice.

TOMB IT MAY CONCERN

Lizzie Borden Tombstone
The small headstone reads "Lizbeth."
Her mother and father are buried nearby.
Oak Grove Cemetery
756 Prospect Street
Fall River, MA

Michigan

The state may be shaped like a mitten, but the "Crime Scene" designation definitely fits like a glove. From missing union bosses to none-too-bright lonely hearts killers to nursing home killers, you'll find them here in the Wolverine State.

BLOOMFIELD TOWNSHIP

THE STORY: *"Union Boss Vanishes Before Last Supper, Never Seen Again"*—1975

 In 1975, Jimmy Hoffa, whose leadership of the Teamsters made him one of the most controversial figures in American labor history, had just been released from a four-year prison sentence for fraud and jury tampering. Now that he was out, he was planning to regain the union presidency, despite resistance from his old colleagues.

On July 30, 1975, he was in the parking lot of the **Machus Red Fox Restaurant** to meet reputed mob leaders Anthony Giacalone and Anthony "Tony Pro" Provenzano.

Witnesses have reported seeing him get into a maroon Mercury with several other men. After the car drove away, he was never seen again.

Despite one of the most intensive FBI investigations in history, no trace has ever been found.

Investigators believe Hoffa was murdered by elements of organized crime to avoid a divisive union fight against Teamsters President Frank Fitzsimmons, or to neutralize his threats to reveal details of the mob's involvement in the union and millions of dollars in unsecured loans to organized crime figures from the union's pension funds.

However, no body, no crime. So no one knows what really happened. Most of the witnesses are gone now, too. Provenzano, a major New Jersey mob figure and Teamsters official, died in prison. There is no proof that Provenzano ever met with Hoffa that day.

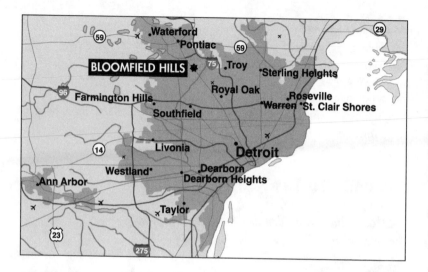

THE SCENE:

Machus Red Fox Restaurant Site
6676 Telegraph Road
Bloomfield Hills, MI

Say, Elvis, Have You Seen Jimmy Hoffa?

At 24 years, the search for Jimmy Hoffa has become one of the most exhaustive investigations in FBI history.

Like Elvis, people continue to report seeing him alive long after his official death. Unlike "The King," people are also reporting where they've seen him buried.

Despite tens of thousands of tips, thousands of interviews, and hundreds of searches with scent dogs, helicopters, military aircraft equipped with infrared cameras, and foot searches, no hard burial evidence or confirmed sightings have ever been found. The investigation remains open.

A live Jimmy Hoffa has been seen:

* Browsing magazines in a Sav-On Drugstore at Maple and Telegraph in Birmingham, Michigan, late in the afternoon on the day he disappeared.

- Drunk, checking into Room 108 of the Toledo Turnpike Motel, in Toledo, Ohio, using the name "Jewell." The hotel clerk who made the report also said he was alone, driving an American Motors Co. Ambassador with New Jersey plates, paid with cash, and later complained about the noisy fan.
- Living on a farm outside Chattanooga, Tennessee, owned by defendants in a Teamster-related car dealership bombing case.
- Boating on Michigan's Lake St. Clair (as opposed to swimming with the fishes in Lake St. Clair).

At the same time, Jimmy Hoffa's remains reportedly lay:
- Under the west endzone of Giants Stadium at the Meadowlands in East Rutherford, New Jersey.
- Under a field in Woodstock Township in Lenawee County, Michigan.
- In a 100-acre gravel pit owned by Jimmy Hoffa's brother William near Highland on the Oakland-Livingston County border.
- At the bottom of a swimming pool behind a Bloomfield Hills mansion near Turtle Lake.
- Out in the middle of Lake Michigan.
- At the end of a dirt road in the Arctic Circle.
- Under or in just about every freeway, bridge, or major building erected in southeast Michigan since 1975.

Be On the LookOut (BOLO): Serial Killer Alert!!!

"The Babysitter": This killer preyed on suburban Detroit children only when it snowed, then took meticulous care of the victims while they were held captive only to murder them using different methods.

During the winter of 1976, six children disappeared in the Oakland County area. Four of their corpses had been cleaned obsessively, then carefully arranged in fresh snow to be found.

The killer has never been caught. But the killings finally stopped, causing authorities to hope that the killer has moved to a much warmer climate.

Minnesota

Like its western neighbor, North Dakota, the North Star State is just too cold for really spectacular crime. That's why creators of the Academy Award-winning movie *Fargo* had to invent the crime that the film was based on.

Despite the cold, there are still a few noteworthy crime scenes here.

Be On the LookOut (BOLO):
Serial Killer Alert!!!

"The Twin Cities Killer": From 1986 to 1994 up to 34 corpses turned up on the streets of the Twin Cities. Most of them were prostitutes in their twenties and thirties who were mutilated, dismembered, and several were decapitated. The killing methods were varied enough for authorities to suspect that it might be the work of more than a single serial killer. To date, no arrests have been made.

NORTHFIELD

THE STORY: *"The James Gang Makes Its Last Raid"—1876*

 Eight heavily armed members of the Jesse James Gang rode into town for an easy bank robbery on September 7, 1876. Jesse and Frank James, Cole Younger and his brother, and four others had come to help themselves to the town's money, as they had done in so many banks in Kansas and Missouri. Without a pause, they shot the bank's cashier in the head when he refused to open the safe.

With the shot, the cry went up, "Get your guns, boys, they're robbing the bank!" And the townsfolk of Northfield did something the James Gang had never encountered before: they fought back. Seven minutes of sustained gunfire later, a legendary gang of outlaws had been handed a

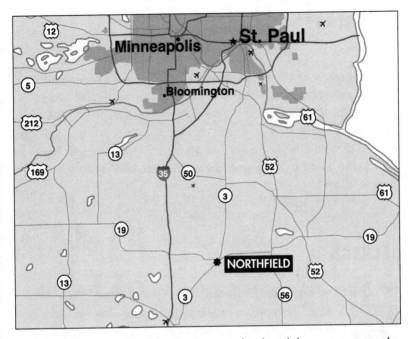

very bitter defeat: Two of the gang were dead and the rest were on the run and, to their embarrassment, empty-handed.

For the next ten days the predators became the prey as the gang was harried relentlessly across the state. One member of the gang died in an ambush in Madelia. Cole Younger, his two brothers, and another gang member were captured after another shootout and sent to prison. Only Frank and Jesse James, who'd split from the gang earlier, escaped on September 17 by riding into South Dakota.

THE SCENE:

James Gang Robbery Site (Northfield Historical Museum)
Scriver Building
408 Division Street
Northfield, MN
507-645-9268

Pick up a self-guided tour of the path the gang took (known as The Outlaw Trail) in their attempt to escape the law.

Mississippi

There's plenty of crime to write home about from the Magnolia State, with hate crimes related to the 1960s civil rights struggle, and more. The state has been reopening and reprosecuting several of the civil rights cases lately, so the crime scenes have even more relevance. It's no wonder that the state is home to Thomas Harris, creator of *The Silence of the Lambs'* Hannibal Lecter and Clarice Starling, and legal thriller writer John Grisham.

So come set a spell.

JACKSON

THE STORY: *"Civil Rights Leader Gunned Down Outside Home"—1963*

 Medgar Evers was a very brave and determined man. Despite the risks, in 1954 he moved his family to Jackson and became the NAACP's first field secretary in Mississippi, organizing voter registration drives, sit-ins, and boycotts to desegregate public facilities.

In 1963, with the voting rights movement well under way, Evers frequently received death threats. On June 2, his house was firebombed. Luckily, no one was injured.

Shortly after midnight on June 12, Evers, 37, was shot in the back as he walked into his house. Only hours before, President Kennedy had given a televised speech declaring a "moral crisis" and calling for civil rights legislation.

After the killing, investigators found a 1917 Enfield rifle in the bushes near the Evers house that was owned by white segregationist Byron de la Beckwith. His fingerprints were on the scope.

At the first trial in 1964, the all-white jury deadlocked and a mistrial was declared after Beckwith claimed his rifle had been stolen and two police officers said they'd seen him at a gas station two hours from Jackson shortly before the shooting. The retrial ended the same way and Beckwith was released. And that was it.

In 1990 after the Jackson *Clarion-Ledger* and the Jackson district attorney's office found new evidence, Beckwith, 70, was retried and convicted. He is currently serving what will effectively be a life sentence.

The 1996 film *Ghosts of Mississippi* was based on a biography of the same name written by Medgar Evers' wife, Myrlie Evers-Williams.

THE SCENE:

Medgar Evers' House
2332 Guynes Street
Jackson, MS

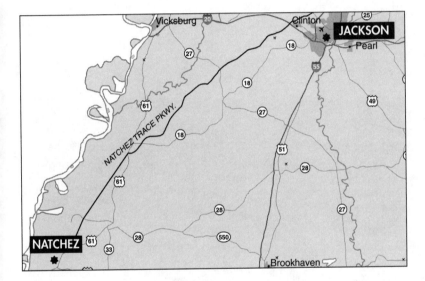

NATCHEZ

THE STORY: *"Madam Killed by Scandalized Son"—1850s*

One of Natchez's prostitutes worked hard to protect her baby boy from the life she knew. She saved, bought a house, became prosperous, and sent her son off to the finest boarding schools and, ultimately, college. When he returned and realized how his mother had put him through college, he was so scandalized he went into a rage and killed her.

Employees at **John Martin's Restaurant,** which now occupies the building, report hearing screams and unexplainable noises from the unoccupied upper floors.

The historian at the Historic Natchez Foundation is familiar with the story, but can't confirm its validity. Natchez-Under-The-Hill was so wild, though, the story could easily be true.

THE SCENE:

John Martin's Restaurant
21 Silver Street
Natchez, MS 39120
601-445-0605

Be On the LookOut (BOLO): *Serial Killer Alert!!!*

"The Columbus Senior Slayer": Five senior citizen victims have been found bound, gagged, and murdered within a three-mile radius in this northeastern timber and manufacturing town. Three of the five victims were strangled and two were stabbed. All were killed in their homes by someone who did not force their way in. In one of the murders, the killer returned to the scene, untied the victim, and set fire to the house.

The crimes were so shocking that the chief of police, a 17-year veteran of law enforcement, immediately formed a task force with police from surrounding jurisdictions and called in the FBI's profiling unit so as not to waste any time in catching the killer.

There is a $250,000 reward for information leading to an arrest of the killer(s). Please contact the Columbus police (601-328-3735) or the local Crimestoppers information line (662-429-8477).

Missouri

Welcome to Jesse James Country! America's best-known Robin Hood made Missouri his habitat, a tradition that other legendary killers continued for decades.

The Show Me State was a peerless place to be if you were a criminal in the 1940s, especially Kansas City. Corruption was rampant and machine-gun artists like Pretty Boy Floyd, Vern Miller, and others flourished.

Calling All Cars! Museum Alert!

Jesse James Farm and Museum
21216 Jesse James Farm Road
Kearney, MO 64060
816-628-6065

America's most famous outlaw, Jesse James, went from farmer to Confederate guerilla at age 16. After the Civil War, he became America's first bank robber and an outlaw legend.

This is where you'll see the dashing outlaw's guns, birth bed, coffin, and remnants of the bomb thrown at his gang by Pinkerton detectives. Unfortunately, the bomb killed several nearby children instead of the outlaws, which only increased sympathy for Jesse and his brother, Frank.

INDEPENDENCE

THE STORY: *"Doctor Murders Wealthy In-laws To Get Family Fortune"—1909*

It was a storybook love affair. Tall, good-looking Dr. Bennett Clarke Hyde was married to Frances Swope, the niece of Thomas Swope, the richest man in Kansas City. Hyde became the family's medical adviser and the couple moved into **the Swope's huge mansion**.

To get at the family's money, Hyde slowly poisoned James Hunton, an old family friend who was also the executor of Thomas Swope's will and estate, and the senior Swope, then attributed their deaths to "apoplexy."

Four of the five nephews and nieces who inherited Swope's fortune were soon stricken by typhoid. One of them died, while the rest recovered.

Finally becoming suspicious, investigators soon discovered that Hyde had murdered Hunton and Swope with a clever mixture of strychnine and cyanide, which the doctor knew would mask the symptoms of the other.

The next Trial of the Century followed on February 9, 1910. Newspapers titillated readers with lurid tales of Hyde trying to murder his way to the family fortune. Through it all, only Frances believed in Hyde's innocence, even after testimony proved that Hyde had received the poisons and a typhoid culture.

After a month-long trial, Hyde was convicted and sentenced to a life term. His trusting wife hired platoons of attorneys who finally sprang Hyde on a technicality.

Dr. Hyde was released and went to live with his wife. He no longer practiced medicine. Ten years later, the ultra-loyal Mrs. Hyde abruptly left her husband after she complained of a stomachache and he offered to make a "special medicine" for her.

THE SCENE:

Swope Family Mansion
The northwest corner of Pleasant and Pacific
Independence, MO

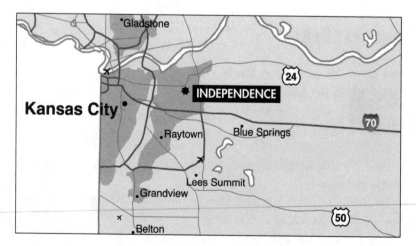

Montana

It should surprise no one to learn that they do crime really big here in Big Sky Country, an area that prizes individual freedom so highly it only recently enacted a speed limit.

The Treasure State has attracted anarchist Ted Kaczynski, the secessionist "Freemen," and the self-styled "Mountain Men" who literally *took* an Olympic athlete as a wife. It also drew Norma Jean Almodovar, the former Los Angeles cop and call girl who has opened a museum of prostitution in Butte.

BIG SKY

THE STORY: *"Olympic Skier Kidnapped as Wife for Mountain Man"*—1984

 On July 15, Olympic biathlon (cross-country skiing, precision riflery) hopeful Kari Swenson was abducted at gunpoint outside the **Big Sky Ski Resort** parking lot while on a training run by two scruffy-looking self-proclaimed "Mountain Men" with long, greasy hair. The older one, Don Nichols, wanted Swenson as a wife for his accomplice, his son Dan. The story, and the months-long search in the Montana wilderness for the Nicholses was the basis for the 1987 TV-movie, *The Abduction of Kari Swenson* starring Tracy Pollan (a.k.a. Mrs. Michael J. Fox).

The Nicholses kept Swenson prisoner for 18 hours, tormenting her most of the time while she was chained to a felled tree. Don Nichols shot Alan Goldstein, a friend of Kari's and member of the search party looking for her, when he stepped into the clearing where she was being held. A .22-caliber rifle bullet also pierced one of Swenson's lungs. After the shooting, the Nicholses abandoned Swenson and fled into the woods. She remained chained to the tree, the body of her friend next to her, for several more hours before being rescued.

Five months later, Montana lawman Johnny France finally captured the Nicholses. The father and son remain in prison in Montana. Montana's current governor, Marc Racicot, was the prosecutor in the trial.

THE SCENE:

Big Sky Ski and Summer Resort
1 Lone Mountain Trail
Big Sky, MT
406-995-5000

LINCOLN

THE STORY: *"Hermit Revealed As Unabomber"—1997*

 Ted Kaczynski, the former Harvard math professor known as the Unabomber, had his cabin here. Though the actual cabin, which was evidence in the trial, now resides on an off-limits part of an Air Force base in California, you can still see where the cabin used to sit. Summer is the best time to visit this very primitive mountain-pass road.

The cabin was located off Stemple Road. Take the Forest Service road to Stemple Pass, about 3 miles out of Lincoln. Stemple Road is located on Hwy 200 in Lincoln. There is one blinking light in the middle of town, which is the intersection of Stemple Road.

Tips: (1) Be polite if you ask for directions. (2) DO NOT TRESPASS. Be sure to ask for permission before you go onto the property. It's private property. They don't get a lot of strangers and everyone is well-armed.

FOR MORE INFORMATION, PLEASE CONTACT:
Lincoln Chamber of Commerce
P.O. Box 985
Lincoln, MT 59639
406-362-4949

Nebraska

The Cornhusker State has an unusual relationship with death and crime. The U.S. Strategic Air Command (the people who make the instantaneous delivery of nuclear weapons a peaceful profession) is based here, and Omaha is the universal hub of telemarketing because it's located in a centralized time zone and the local accent is fairly generic and easy to understand.

Unfortunately, some of the state's crimes aren't so easy to understand.

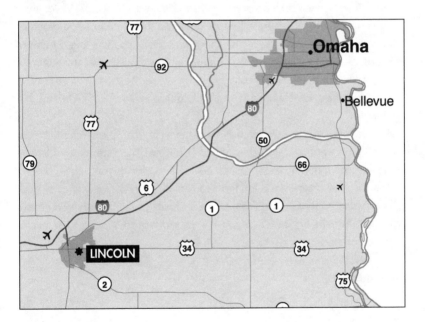

LINCOLN

THE STORY: *"Teenage Couple Kill 11 in Weeklong Murder Rampage"—1958*

Charles Starkweather, also known as Little Red, was a slight, 5'2" redheaded troublemaker. At age 17, he was also a garbageman who idolized James Dean and carried a rifle everywhere he went.

Starkweather's murder spree began on December 1, 1957, with a gas station robbery and killing in Lincoln.

It continued on January 21, 1958, after Starkweather shot the parents of his 14-year-old girlfriend, Caril Ann Fugate. Fugate then watched Starkweather choke her 2-year-old sister to death with the barrel of his rifle.

Fugate went back to watching TV, while Starkweather concealed the bodies and made some sandwiches.

The teen lovers stayed in the house for a week after posting a sign that read, "Stay a Way. Every Body is Sick With the Flu," before leaving to cut a murderous swath across the plains states, killing eight more people unlucky enough to cross their path before they were captured in Douglas, Wyoming.

At their capture and subsequent trial, Fugate tried to pioneer a defense that Patty Hearst would use twenty-five years later: claiming she'd been a hostage all along. It didn't work then either. She drew a life sentence and was paroled in the late 1970s.

Starkweather was electrocuted at midnight June 24, 1959. He was 19 years old.

True to form, when asked to donate his eyes for transplant after the execution, Starkweather refused, saying, "Hell, no! No one ever did anything for me! Why the hell should I do anything for anyone else?"

Their story was the basis for Terence Malick's 1973 film *Badlands* and Oliver Stone's 1994 movie *Natural Born Killers*. Bruce Springsteen based the title song of his 1982 acoustic album *Nebraska* on a first-person account of the Badlands spree.

THE SCENE:

Charles Starkweather Grave
Wyuka Cemetery
3600 O Street
Lincoln, NB
402-474-3600

In Wyuka Cemetery in Lincoln, find the R Street entrance. Starkweather is in section 28, which is the first section to your left coming in on R Street. The gravesite is about 18 lotsites north of (directly behind) the section 28 marker.

Nevada

The Old West meets the New West and the result is a state where gambling and prostitution are legal (statewide for the former and in 10 of 17 counties for the latter); TV's Ponderosa Ranch is a real place; and mobsters are required to take their murders elsewhere because it's bad for business (to wit, Bugsy Siegel may have invented Las Vegas as we know it, but he was murdered in Beverly Hills, California).

Suffice it to say that Lady Luck is just waiting for crime scene fans.

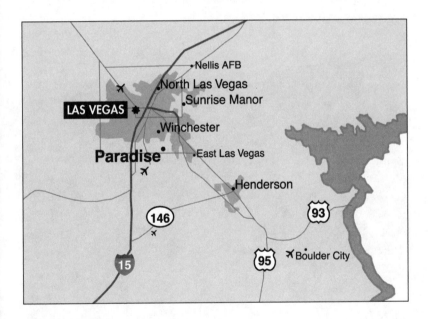

LAS VEGAS

THE STORY: *"Casino Heir's Death Ruled Murder, Not Suicide"—1998*

 Ted Binion, eccentric son of the man who opened the **Horseshoe Club**, a downtown Las Vegas landmark since the 1940s, was found dead here on September 17, 1998. Because Binion had a long history of drug abuse, finding an

empty bottle of Xanax next to his body and lethal levels of the prescription sedative and heroin in his system made suicide seem extremely likely.

But in March 1999, when police caught three men digging up millions of dollars' worth of silver coins and bars that Binion had buried in the desert, enough to overload a dump truck, the death was reinvestigated and ruled a murder.

Though no one has been charged yet, newspapers report that police are looking closely at Binion's 26-year-old live-in girlfriend, Sandy Murphy, and the contractor who'd built the underground vault. He was one of the men arrested with Binion's silver.

There is one small footnote. Sandy Murphy's attorney is David Chesnoff, law partner of Las Vegas's new mayor, Oscar Goodman.

THE HORSESHOE—WHERE BINION'S LUCK RAN OUT.

THE SCENES:

Ted Binion's House
2408 Palomino Lane
Las Vegas, NV

Binion's Horseshoe Hotel and Casino
128 East Fremont Street
Las Vegas, NV
702-382-1600
800-634-6811

PAHRUMP

THE STORY: *"Pistol-packing Granny Rids Town of Crime"—1970s*

 The feud between local brothel owners raged for years, escalating into a 1978 arson fire that consumed the independently run **Chicken Ranch**.

Fed up with the feuding and the corruption, Joni Wines, a white-haired grandma, set out to clean up her little corner of the Old West. She quickly unseated incumbent Nye County Sheriff C.J. Howard in an election soon after the Chicken Ranch fire. The pistol-packing lady sheriff then took steps to end the "Nye County Brothel Wars."

Wines hired two aggressive investigators who collected enough evidence about the fire to have four local men, including a Nye County brothel owner, indicted by a federal grand jury.

Unfortunately, local residents were upset by Wines' methods and voted to recall her a few months afterward. Wines later ran unsuccessfully for governor, Congress, the state Senate, and Assembly.

The bordello was named after the original Chicken Ranch in Texas, which was the basis for the hit musical *The Best Little Whorehouse in Texas* and the feature film that starred Burt Reynolds and Dolly Parton.

THE SCENE:

The Chicken Ranch
10511 Homestead Road (call for directions)
Pahrump, NV 89041
702-382-7870

New Hampshire

Solid as a rock, the Granite State opts for quality, not quantity, when it comes to crime scenes.

The state had the fourth lowest murder rate in 1994, which must be what attracted Jean Harris. She moved to the state after being granted clemency in December 1992 after serving 12 years for shooting her lover, Dr. Herman Tarnower, author of the best-selling Scarsdale diet book.

DERRY

THE STORY: *"High School Teacher Seduces Student into Murder"—1990*

 The murder itself was horrible. On May 1, a few days before his first wedding anniversary, 24-year-old Gregory Smart was killed with a single shot from a .38 revolver when he arrived home at the couple's condo and interrupted a burglary.

The story behind the murder was even worse.

A week later, **Winnacunnet High School** student William Flynn, 15, was arrested as the shooter, along with two other students as accomplices. The

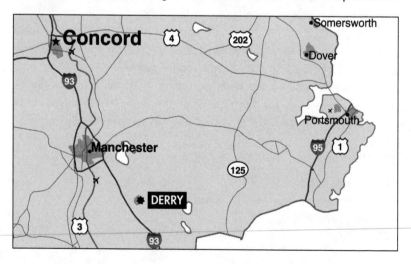

stunning news was the killing had been masterminded by Smart's wife, Pamela, a hometown girl into heavy metal rock and roll, who used a sexual relationship with Flynn to get him to commit the murder. She was also arrested.

Smart's teaching aide, Cecilia Pierce, had caught Smart and her student having sex and plotting to kill Pamela's husband. Pierce later wore a wire during a conversation in which Smart confessed.

While in jail at the **Bedford Hills Correctional Facility**, Smart tried to arrange to have another inmate kill Pierce. Flynn was convicted of murder and is serving 28 years to life. Convicted of conspiracy to commit murder, accomplice to first-degree murder, and witness-tampering, Smart was considered a contract killer, no different from the Mafiosi who traditionally commit these crimes. She received a life sentence without the possibility of parole.

In 1996, Smart, whose favorite song is Van Halen's "Hot For Teacher," won a scholarship from the University of Alabama to study criminal justice from prison. According to Smart's attorney, she received the grant because the school felt she had a "unique position" to analyze the judicial system.

Following the scholarship, Smart filed an appeal claiming that, among other things: the teenage boys who killed her husband were the real masterminds and they framed her; and her life sentence was "cruel and unusual" because the then-15-year-old boy who actually committed the murder only got a 28-year sentence.

The appeal was thrown out.

1995's *To Die For,* starring Nicole Kidman, was based on this story.

THE SCENES:

The Smarts' House
4E Misty Morning Drive
Derry, NH

Winnacunnet High School
4 Alumni Drive
Hampton, NH

Bedford Hills Correctional Facility
Harris Road
Bedford Hills, NH
603-241-3100

New Jersey

There's more to crime here than just burying the overflow from New York City's mob hits.

The Garden State is the site of one of the true crimes (the Lindbergh baby kidnapping) and trials of the century (Bruno Richard Hauptmann). It is also the site of the biggest "Trial of the Century" before the O.J. Simpson trial.

HOPEWELL

THE STORY: *"Aviation Pioneer Lindbergh's Baby Kidnapped!"—1932*

 All anyone knows for certain is that on March 1, 1932, the infant son of Charles Lindbergh was kidnapped from his upstairs bedroom and a ransom note for $50,000 was left at the scene. A homemade ladder was left outside the window to the baby's room.

Two months later, the boy's body was found in a shallow grave.

In 1934, Bruno Richard Hauptmann, a German immigrant, was arrested for the crime. A year later, in the de rigueur Trial of the Century, he was tried, mostly in the press, convicted, and executed. The house is now a residential center for boys and not open to the public. You can contact the program superintendent, though, to ask about tours of the house.

THE SCENE:

The Lindberghs' House (now the Albert Ellis Residential Group Center)
188 Lindbergh Road
Hopewell, NJ 08525

Calling All Cars! Museum Alert!

New Jersey State Prison
Cass Street
Trenton, NJ

Visit the home of "Smokey," the state's electric chair. Bruno Hauptmann was electrocuted here.

Be On the LookOut (BOLO): *Serial Killer Alert!!!*

Since 1993, the stabbed, strangled, or suffocated bodies of 14 African-American women, many of them prostitutes, have been found in vacant lots or abandoned buildings within a few miles from each other in the Newark, Irvington, and East Orange areas. They were between 19 and 37 years old.

Though the women were killed in different ways and disposed of in different places, a high-ranking law enforcement source told *The Newark Star-Ledger*, "All indications point to a serial killer." There are no suspects at this time.

SOMERVILLE

THE STORY: *"Minister and Mistress Murdered, Minister's Wife Suspected"—1922*

It was the Trial of the Century that preceded the Lindbergh baby kidnapping. On September 16, 1922, the brutalized bodies of local minister Edward Hall, 41, and Eleanor Mills, 34, were found in a local lover's lane. Both had been shot. Mills' throat had been slashed and her tongue and voicebox had been removed. Around the bodies, investigators found torn-up love letters and the minister's calling card propped against one of his feet.

Hall's 48-year-old wife Frances and her brothers Willie and Henry were suspected, but there was insufficient evidence to proceed.

In 1927, the case was reopened when prosecutors learned that Hall's maid, Louise Geist, knew about Edward's plans to elope with Eleanor and told Frances. On the night of the murder, Geist said she drove out to the lane with Frances and her brother Willie and participated in the killings. Frances mutilated Eleanor's throat to remove the sweet voice that had stolen her husband's affections.

The Hall-Mills murder trial was a sensational and sensationalized affair. In addition to Geist, the other star witness was Jane Gibson, known in print as "The Pig Woman," because she overheard the murder while out tending to her pig farm. Gibson's mother testified that her daughter was a pathological liar. Gibson, who had end-stage cancer, collapsed several times and finally had to give her testimony from a hospital bed.

The smoking gun was brother Willie's full fingerprint, which was found on Edward's calling card. Three top fingerprint experts confirmed the identification.

However, since fingerprint evidence was new (it was the 1920s counterpart to DNA identification), defense attorney Robert McCarter employed the early 1920s precursor to Johnnie Cochran's appeal to ignorance, "If the glove doesn't fit, you must acquit," telling the jury, "I charge with all the solemnity that is involved in it that the card is a fraud."

And that was good enough for the jury, which ignored the case facts and quickly acquitted everyone.

Historians believe that another critical factor in the acquittal was the case prosecutor who alienated the jury from the start by referring to local residents as "country bumpkins." Most believe that the verdict was more a gesture of contempt for the prosecutor than an affirmation of the defendants' innocence.

New Mexico

Welcome to Billy the Kid country.

Though no one's sure whether his real name was William H. Bonney, Henry Antrim, or Henry McCarty, or where he was born (sparse records suggest that it's most likely New York City), what is certain is that this mercurial, back-shooting mass murdering legend is one of the Land of Enchantment's favorite sons. Go figure.

It's hard to believe that the most feared gunman in the West was a skinny kid who barely had fuzz on his cheeks.

Calling All Cars! Museum Alert!

Historical Museum of Lawmen
Dona Ana County Sheriff's Office lobby
1725 Marquess Street
Las Cruces, NM 88001
505-525-1911

In 1895, Pat Garrett, the legendary lawman who shot Billy the Kid, was appointed sheriff of Dona Ana County. You can now see his roll-top desk. You can also see the ledger showing where Pat Garrett was killed, and where his killer was arrested. Historical photographs of the late 19th century lawman, weapons, badges, handcuffs, brass knuckles, and lots more can be seen in this display which is located in the Sheriff's Office lobby.

Historic Lincoln Courthouse Museum
Lincoln State Monument
Hwy 380 in Lincoln
Lincoln, NM 88338

The site of Billy's desperate April 28 jailbreak, the four buildings in the Lincoln Courthouse Museum house artifacts from most of The Kid's short life in and around the area, including the Lincoln County War, where Billy avenged the murder of his mentor, John Tunstall, and acquired most of the notches on his gun.

TOMB IT MAY CONCERN

Billy the Kid's Tombstone
Fort Sumner Cemetery
The Fort Sumner State Monument
Billy the Kid Road
Fort Sumner, NM

Billy, age 22, was buried with his friends, Tom O'Folliard and Charlie Bowdre. The stone over this grave bears the names of its three occupants and the word "Pals." The gravestone is in the old cemetery outside the Fort Sumner city limits.

SOCORRO

THE STORY: *"Teenage Lawman Survives New Mexico's Most Famous Gunfight"—1884*

At the callow age of 19, mercantile clerk and self-styled deputy, Elfego Baca, a Socorro native, became a folk hero when he held off 50 heavily armed cattlemen in a fierce two-day gun battle in the town of San Francisco Plaza, New Mexico (commonly known as Frisco, later renamed Reserve).

The gunfight was set in motion after Baca, in lieu of a sheriff, apprehended a cowboy who was "hurrahing" the town by shooting at the

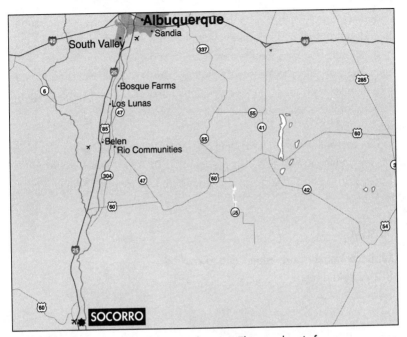

Mexican residents to get them to "dance." The cowboy's foreman, a man named Perham, protested and tried to intimidate Baca with a crowd of cowboys. After warning the cowboys to disperse, Baca began firing, wounding one cowboy in the knee, hitting Perham's horse, and mortally injuring the foreman.

The next day, Baca suddenly found himself facing all the employees of the ranch, led by its revenge-seeking rancher, the ironically named Tom Slaughter. For the next 24 hours, Baca holed up in a tiny mud hut while his attackers shot at him from the safety of an adobe churchyard wall. He returned fire through a small gap near the floor with deadly accuracy. During the siege, the frustrated cattlemen tried lobbing in dynamite sticks and rushing the hut using iron cookstoves as shields, only to sustain more casualties.

As the sun rose the next day, Baca was seen calmly cooking his breakfast in the ruins of the hut. The townspeople cheered and the battle resumed.

By the time deputies arrived to stop the fight, Baca had killed a handful of cowboys and wounded many more—without sustaining a scratch.

The survivor of New Mexico's most famous gunfight was a popular figure who was elected to many public offices in the area by landslides, including deputy sheriff, county sheriff, mayor of Socorro, school superintendent, and district attorney. He was nearly elected governor, too.

As sheriff, Baca frequently used his fearsome reputation instead of his gun. He sent letters to the area's meanest desperadoes, advising them to turn themselves in or find themselves on the receiving end of his six-guns. Several of these fearsome killers promptly appeared at the jail to be taken into custody.

The famous lawman was immortalized in a "Wonderful World of Disney" multi-part TV-movie in the late 1950s, *The Nine Lives of Elfego Baca*, starring Robert Loggia as a kinder, gentler version of the legendary gunfighter.

THE SCENE:

J.J. Baca House, store where Elfego clerked
112 Abeyta Street
Socorro, NM

New York

New York City has been a haven for crime since Peter Minuit bought Manhattan Island from the Manhattan tribe of the Wappinger Confederacy Native Americans for $24 worth of beads.

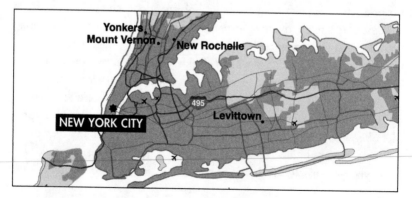

Today, New York City is the supermarket of sin, a veritable Crime-opolis. If humans can do it, they've done it here—repeatedly. But there's more to New York than New York City. For convicted criminals, the legendary upstate prison is where the phrase, "being sent up the (Hudson) river," originated. For crime scene fans, the prison means "Of thee I Sing Sing."

WHODUNIT HOTEL

The Helmsley Palace Hotel
455 Madison Avenue
New York, NY
212-888-7000

After marrying hotel king Harry Helmsley, Leona Helmsley anointed herself "Queen." She starred herself in a major ad campaign for the hotel with a theme built around her regal attitude and her short imperial fuse for imperfect service—"The Only Palace in the World Where the Queen Stands Guard." After her tax fraud conviction, in which she said, "I don't pay taxes. The little people pay taxes," the press referred to her prison as the only palace in the world where "The Queen" has a guard.

Calling All Cars! Museum Alert!

New York State Prison (Sing Sing)
354 Hunter Street
Ossining, NY
914-941-0108

The up-the-river destination for the state's most notorious criminals and killers, Sing Sing is also the home of the state's electric chair.

Electrical pioneer George Westinghouse was shocked by the barbarity of the electric chair. After seeing it used, he commented, "They would have done better with an axe!"

At 66, killer cannibal Albert Fish was the oldest man to die in Sing Sing's electric chair. The chair has been retired in favor of lethal injection for decades.

NEW YORK CITY

THE STORY: *"Homicidal Nerd Assassinates John Lennon"—1980*

 It was the nerd fantasy come true. Mark David Chapman was a nobody who wanted to be somebody. So on December 8, 1980, he joined the crowd of Beatles fans lingering outside **The Dakota** apartment building, where John Lennon lived. At 5 P.M., as Lennon left home for The Hit Factory recording studio, he stopped to autograph Chapman's copy of the *Double Fantasy* record album. At 11 P.M. when Lennon returned, Chapman jumped out of the courtyard shadows, yelled, "Hey, John!" and fired his .38-caliber pistol. Two slugs ripped into Lennon's back and spun him around. Chapman fired two more into Lennon's upper body, killing the rock legend.

When the police arrived minutes later, they found Lennon's wife, Yoko Ono, screaming and Chapman standing nearby calmly reading *The Catcher in the Rye.*

Chapman received a life sentence and will be eligible for parole in 2001.

THE DAKOTA, ON THE CORNER
OF 72ND AND CENTRAL PARK WEST.

At Yoko Ono's urging, a portion of Central Park across from The Dakota has been named **Strawberry Fields** to honor Lennon. Every October 9 and December 8, fans gather there to celebrate Lennon's arrival and passing.

THE SCENES:

The Dakota
1 West 72nd Street
New York, NY

Strawberry Fields
Central Park (near West 72nd
    Street Park entrance)
New York, NY

* * * * * *

THE STORY: *".44-caliber Killer Stalks Streets of New York"—1976*

 Perhaps the most notorious criminal in New York—and that's saying a lot—is David Berkowitz, best known as the "Son of Sam." He liked to shoot pretty women with long hair. The high-powered bullets he used gave the then-unknown Berkowitz his media moniker "The .44-caliber Killer."

After his sixth killing, Berkowitz left a note near the scene addressed to the detective in charge of the investigation, identifying himself as Son of Sam, claiming to be "Beelzebub—the chubby behemouth (sic)" prowling the streets in search of "fair game—tasty meat." To Sam, "the women of Queens are prettyist (sic) of all."

A parking ticket provided the break in the case. Berkowitz had parked illegally to commit one of the crimes. As Berkowitz was being taken into custody, he proudly announced that he was Son of Sam, responsible for killing six and wounding seven. According to his sentencing, he will become eligible for parole in 2002, and his sentence ends in 2007.

Spike Lee's 1999 movie *Summer of Sam* is about the fateful summer when Berkowitz ravaged the city.

THE SCENE:

Son of Sam Arrest Site
42 Pine (35 was the original number, but the owners changed it to
    discourage sightseers.)
Yonkers, NY

THE STORY: *"Headless Body in Topless Bar!"—1983*

 That's the *New York Post's* most famous headline. And here's the story.

On April 14, 1983, a patron was shot during a hold-up in **Herbie's Topless Bar** in Queens. Fearing he'd be identified by the bullet, the gunman ordered a waitress to dig the slug out of the man's skull. When she couldn't find the bullet, he forced her to cut the man's head off with a steak knife, stuff it in a box, then wrap it with streamers torn from a party decoration.

The gunman took the waitress and another woman from the bar and fled. Thinking quickly, the waitress brought along a bottle of liquor from the bar and kept the gunman drinking throughout the wild ride to Manhattan, which ended when the gunman pulled the car over at 168th Street and Broadway and passed out. The women grabbed the car keys and fled, taking a nearby subway train to the 59th Street station at Columbus Circle, where they told transit cops their harrowing story.

Transit cop Fred Mack arrested the gunman, with the boxed head still in the car, as he was beginning to wake up.

This story inspired the 1995 drama/comedy film of the same name from Green Tea Productions.

THE SCENE:

Herbie's Bar (no longer a strip club)
182–41 Jamaica Avenue
Hollis area of Queens
Queens, NY

Perhaps He Was Looking for Another "Hit" from "Panama"—1993

David Lee Roth Drug Bust
Washington Square Park
MacDougal Street and Minetta Lane
New York, NY

On April 16, 1993, former Van Halen singer David Lee Roth, age 38, was arrested for marijuana possession in Washington Square Park after police saw him make a buy. Roth was picked up along with 38 others in a drug sweep at the park.

Roth entered court facing drug possession charges and up to 15 days in jail or a fine of $250.

Despite his reputation for wild on- and off-stage antics, which included flying around the stage on a wire, the judge accepted Roth's word that he'd never committed that crime before and dropped all the charges; his criminal record was wiped clean after he behaved himself for a year.

It was one record the platinum-selling recording artist was happy to have disappear.

THE STORY: *"Julius and Ethel Rosenberg Deliver Atom Bomb Secrets to Russians?"—1950*

 In late 1946, the National Security Agency (NSA) intercepted and broke encrypted cables from the Soviet Consulate to the KGB. The messages, which became known as the "Verona Cables," included a report by British physicist Klaus Fuchs describing progress of the U.S. government's super-secret atomic program, known as the Manhattan Project.

Fuchs had been passing plans for the atomic bomb to a chemist from Philadelphia named Harry Gold. In addition to getting information from Fuchs, Gold had also been sent to Los Alamos by his handler, Anatoli Yakovlev, head of the Russian UN delegation and the KGB's chief of U.S. spy operations. He was told to meet another contact with the password, "I come from Julius." To confirm the recognition, he was to present a jig-sawed half of a Jell-O box. The contact would supply the matching half.

The contact turned out to be David Greenglass, 29, a Manhattan Project machinist from New York City.

On July 17, 1950, on the basis of testimony from Greenglass, the FBI arrested Julius Rosenberg in front of his wife, Ethel, and two sons, Robert, 7, and Michael, 3. Despite what the others had confessed, Julius adamantly denied the charges.

Though there was extremely limited evidence of her guilt, Ethel was arrested on August 11, 1950. Neither she nor Julius ever confessed to spying.

After a dramatic trial, the Rosenbergs were convicted of espionage. Describing their crime as "worse than murder," Judge Irving Kaufman blamed the Rosenbergs for the 50,000 American deaths in Korea and sentenced them to die in the electric chair at Sing Sing Prison.

Despite a very dramatic two-year appeal process that included the Rosenbergs' sons Robert and Michael appearing at protest marches carrying signs reading "Don't Kill My Mommy and Daddy," worldwide support for clemency, and even a letter from the Pope, Julius and Ethel Rosenberg were executed shortly after 8 P.M. on June 19, 1953.

The Rosenbergs were the first Americans convicted and executed for treason in peacetime. Ethel Rosenberg was only the second woman executed by the United States government.

In 1995, after the fall of the Soviet Union, KGB records confirmed Julius's work as a Russian spy—but not for atomic secrets. The records show that Julius gave the Russians a proximity fuse that let them shoot down an American U-2 spy plane in 1960.

Further, according to experts, the Rosenbergs didn't give the Russians anything they didn't already receive from the U.S. government. Usable plans appeared in the 30,000 copies of the U.S. government-published book, *Atomic Energy for Military Purposes* that the Soviet Union received in 1945.

THE SCENES:

The Rosenbergs' home
10 Monroe Street
Knickerbocker Village
New York, NY

Ethel and Julius Rosenberg's Tombstones
Wellwood Cemetery
Pinelawn Road
Farmingdale (Long Island), NY
516-947-5425

Note: Both halves of the infamous Jell-O box are on display in the FBI Museum (see Washington, D.C.).

North Carolina

The Tar Heel State is a tough place to be a doctor. Several doctors failed to diagnose arsenic poisoning, another was sued for malpractice by a patient who went on a shooting rampage, and an Army doctor was convicted of beating his wife and children to death.

BURLINGTON

THE STORY: *"Black Widow's Trail of Poisoning Ends with Minister"*—1989

 A native Tar Heel, Blanche Taylor Moore was the daughter of a self-ordained minister who drank heavily and used the sexual favors of young Blanche to pay off gambling debts. She married James Taylor, a fellow just like her father, and got a job at the **Kroger Supermarket** in Burlington.

For the next 25 years, Blanche became involved in a chain of relationships, meeting a new guy just as the old one was becoming suddenly, terminally, and for her, conveniently, ill.

She was abetted by doctors who seemed unable to diagnose the unique symptoms of arsenic poisoning: violent stomach cramps, diarrhea, projectile vomiting, delirium, and bright-blue face and eyeballs. Instead, they attributed the deaths of her father, her husband, her mother-in-law, and her boyfriend to emphysema, flu, and the rarely-fatal Guillain-Barre syndrome. They were also moved by Blanche's devotion to her "patients," bringing them homemade treats like ice cream and pudding.

Blanche nurtured her father, her first husband, her mother-in-law, and her boyfriend to death this way.

Her last husband became critically ill and nearly died before doctors discovered that he'd ingested twenty times the lethal dose of arsenic—enough to literally kill a moose. Police began exhuming bodies and quickly discovered a trail of arsenic poisoning.

Blanche was tried for Raymond Reid's murder in Winston-Salem on October 21, 1990, and was sentenced on January 18, 1991, to die by lethal injection. As of this writing, she is still appealing.

Elizabeth Montgomery starred in the 1995 TV-movie about the case, *Black Widow Murders: The Blanche Taylor Moore Story.*

THE SCENE:

Kroger Supermarket

1801 South Church Street (in shopping center formerly known as Spoon's Plaza; grocery site most recently occupied by a Lowe's market.)
Burlington, NC

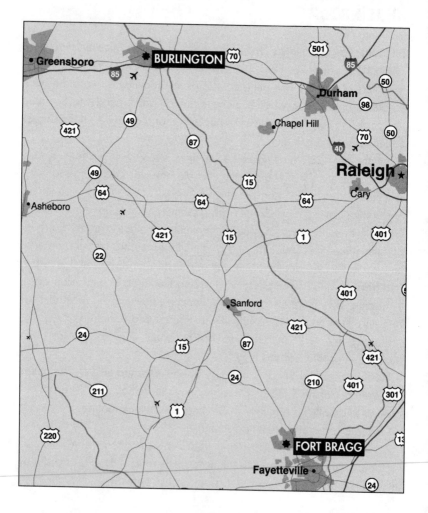

FORT BRAGG

THE STORY: *"Doctor Kills Wife and Daughters, Blames Hippies"—1970*

Jeffrey Robert MacDonald epitomized the all-American boy next door. He worked hard, went to Princeton on a scholarship, married his high school sweetheart, became a doctor, and joined the Army's elite Green Berets. He and his wife had two pretty little girls.

All of that ended suddenly on the night of February 17, 1970, when military police got an urgent call from MacDonald crying, "We've been stabbed! People are dying!" A bleeding MacDonald told the police that four drug-crazed hippies had murdered his wife and daughters, while one held a candle and chanted, "Acid is groovy. Kill the pigs."

What the military police found was a bloodbath. His wife and both daughters had been stabbed dozens of times with a knife and dozens more with an icepick. They'd all been clubbed in the head, shattering their skulls.

In contrast, MacDonald's injury was what doctors later described as a "clean, small, sharp" incision in the right chest that was easily repaired. MacDonald was tried in a civilian criminal court, convicted of the murders, and sentenced to three life terms. The case has been to the U.S. Supreme Court seven times, setting a record for a modern criminal proceeding. In March of 1999, MacDonald appealed for DNA testing of blood, hair, and fiber samples. However, legal wrangling over the samples and the tests are still underway. MacDonald remains in prison.

THE SCENE:

The MacDonalds' House
544 Castle Drive
Fort Bragg, NC

North Dakota

"Forty below keeps the riffraff out," proclaim the natives of subarctic Bismarck. But they could be speaking for the rest of the state too.

North Dakota routinely ranks as having the lowest crime rate in the nation. According to FBI statistics for 1997, the latest year available, North Dakota had the nation's fewest murders (6), the fewest robberies (41), and the lowest state prisoner incarceration rate. Nationally, one out of 167 Americans is in jail. In North Dakota, it's one out of 1,000.

Still, there's at least one attraction for the crime scene visitor.

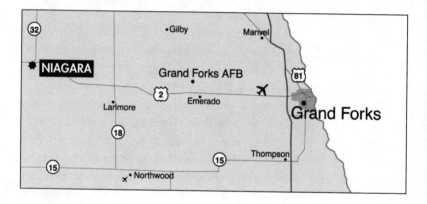

NIAGARA

THE STORY: *"Six Murder Victims Found under Floor"—1915*

Two years after "Eccentric" Eugene Butler died, skeletal remains were found under **his former home outside Niagara**. A paranoid recluse, Butler shunned contact with his fellow man for many years, until he was committed to the asylum at Jamestown in 1906. He died there in 1913.

During an excavation, contractors found six skeletons lined up in shallow graves beneath the floor. The coroner was able to determine that all the victims were male, five were adults, and one was between 15 and 18 years old. All had been killed by crushing blows to the skull over a period of four to five years before Butler was committed.

Without Butler as a suspect or identities of the victims, no one knows exactly who they are or why he killed them. They could have been transient farmhands he murdered in lieu of payment, as Juan Corona did in California fifty years later, or they could have been victims of homosexual violence, like the bodies under John Wayne Gacy's house in Illinois sixty years later (see Des Plaines, Illinois).

THE SCENE:

Eugene Butler's House
Township 152 North-Range 56 West
Niagara, ND

Ohio

Of all the towns in Ohio, Cleveland has been a beacon of innovative law enforcement and brutal crimes.

Famed Untouchable Elliot Ness retired to Cleveland after his Chicago gangbusting days were over and waged war on crime, and, later, VD.

On the other side of the law, Bath is Jeffrey Dahmer's hometown and original killing zone. He killed his first victim there in 1978 at age 18. He didn't kill again for the next eight years.

And in 1970, Kent State proved deadly for a few protesting college students.

CLEVELAND

THE STORY: *"Cleveland Torso Murderer Kills 12 and 'Untouchable' Elliot Ness' Career"—1938*

Also known as "The Mad Butcher of Kingsbury Run" from 1935 to 1938, this maniacal killer decapitated and dissected his victims and was never officially caught. While the official body count

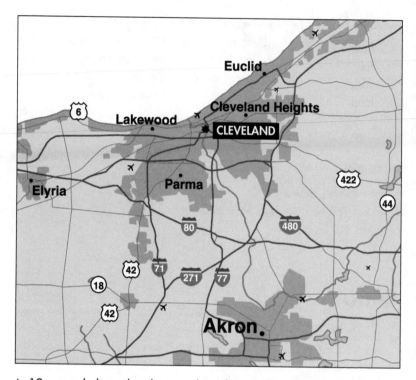

is 12, some believe that the actual number is closer to 40.

The Butcher's sophisticated anatomical knowledge and surgical skills also linked him to the Black Dahlia murder case in Los Angeles (see California).

Elliot Ness, the man who formed and led "The Untouchables," an incorruptible squad of lawmen credited with bringing down Chicago racketeer Al Capone, was on the case but his inability to officially solve it ended his political aspirations. Lacking the lift of another legal triumph, he was unsuccessful in his run for mayor of Cleveland.

According to biographers, Ness believed the Butcher was a medical student from a prominent and politically potent Cleveland family that was able to keep the killer's name unknown. They support this theory with the fact that the murders stopped in August of 1938, after Ness forced the family to institutionalize their student doctor. The story is reinforced by the fact that the killings resumed briefly in 1950 when he was let out, and stopped again when he was returned to the hospital.

THE SCENE:

Cleveland Safety Director Elliot Ness's Office
City Hall
601 Lakeside Avenue
Cleveland, OH 44104

Be On the LookOut (BOLO): Serial Killer Alert!!!

The "Ohio 'Couples' Murderer": Between August 1979 and October 1982, four young Ohio couples (eight victims) were brutally murdered in a triangular death zone formed by Akron, Toledo, and Logan. The evidence suggests there were two killers, but no motive has been found. The murders remain unsolved.

Oklahoma

It's called the Sooner State because many of the original settlers took illegal head starts during the land grant period, staking out their claims *sooner* than the official opening date of April 22, 1889.

In terms of crime scenes, well, the sooner you get here . . .

GUTHRIE

THE STORY: *"Wild West Outlaw Winds Up as California Amusement Park Dummy"—1976*

Elmer McCurdy was a notorious turn-of-the-20th-century safe-cracker, train robber, and killer who was gunned down in a shootout with deputies in March 1911 in the Osage hills. His preserved but unclaimed body was last seen collecting dust in a forgotten corner of a Pawhuska funeral home.

In December 1976, a lighting technician working on an episode of *The Six Million Dollar Man* in a Long Beach, California, amusement park fun house knocked the arm off one of the fiberglass mannequins. The dummy, which was painted luminescent red, dangled at the end of a rope in the gallows. When the technician went to glue the arm back on, he saw a bone inside and realized it was human.

Working back from a 1924 penny and a few old ticket stubs found lodged down the mummy's throat, investigators from the L.A. County Coroner's office identified the body and traced its bizarre path to Long Beach.

After he died, McCurdy's body was displayed in a traveling oddities show and later wound up in a defunct crime museum in L.A. The remains were then sold to the Hollywood Wax Museum along with the rest of the museum's holdings when the crime museum closed. The wax museum determined that McCurdy's body wasn't "life-like" enough, so they sold it to the amusement park.

McCurdy's remains are now buried at **Summit View**, near other famous Oklahoma outlaws.

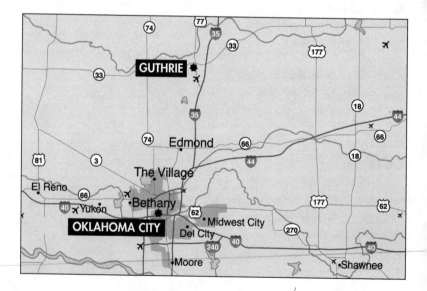

THE SCENE:

Elmer McCurdy's Grave
Summit View Cemetery
1808 North Pine
Guthrie, OK
405-282-2773

OKLAHOMA CITY

THE STORY: *"Oklahoma City Federal Building Bombed, 168 Killed"—1995*

On the morning of April 19, 1995, a rental truck filled with an ammonium nitrate fertilizer bomb exploded in front of the **Alfred P. Murrah Federal Building**. Amazingly, a handheld tape recorder being used in a nearby office at the time for dictation captured the noise and the terror.

One hundred sixty-eight people died. Many more were injured. Major portions of the massive building ceased to exist.

After a sweeping investigation, Army buddies and white supremacist hate group members Timothy McVeigh and Terry Nichols were soon arrested. They were later tried in Denver. McVeigh received a death sentence and currently resides on the new federal Death Row in Terre Haute, Indiana. Nichols received a life sentence. Under federal law there is no parole. Unless Nichols' conviction or sentence is overturned, he will never leave prison alive.

Construction of a 24,000-square-foot memorial center on the site of the Murrah Federal Building began in January 1999. To help visitors relate to the horror, the memorial will feature several multimedia elements, such as the rushing roar of the bomb exploding and the faces of the victims. There will also be interactive stations where guests can view news coverage and listen to stories from survivors and those who responded to the emergency. A memorial registry will allow visitors to leave messages for the people of Oklahoma City.

THE SCENE:

Alfred P. Murrah Building
Oklahoma City National Memorial Center
Located between Robinson Street and Harvey Avenue and 4th and 6th streets.
Oklahoma City, OK
888-542-4673

Calling All Cars! Museum Alert!

Oklahoma Prisons Historical Museum
Corner of West and Stonewall Streets
P.O. Box 97
McAlester, OK 74502
918-423-4700

Oklahoma State Penitentiary (a.k.a. "Big Mac") has been home for many of the state's most incorrigible lawbreakers since the days of the Wild West. Guests include Butch Cassidy and The Sundance Kid, Nanny Doss, and Elmer McCurdy. The museum chronicles this rich inmate history. It's open on Wednesday mornings (8:45–11:45), but tours can be arranged for other times if you call ahead.

TULSA

THE STORY: *"'Giggling Grandma' Poisons 10, Probably More"—1954*

Getting on Nanny Hazel Doss's nerves could be fatal. It was for two of her children, her only grandchild, her mother, both of her sisters, and four of her five husbands—before she was caught.

The pattern was so simple, it's hard to believe it took so long to detect. People were healthy until Nanny Doss arrived. Robustly well people suddenly fell ill after Nanny's hospitality and all soon succumbed to "mysterious cramps" followed by convulsions, then death. Police later learned that she'd fed them all stewed prunes dosed with her secret ingredient—a mixture of rat poison and arsenic.

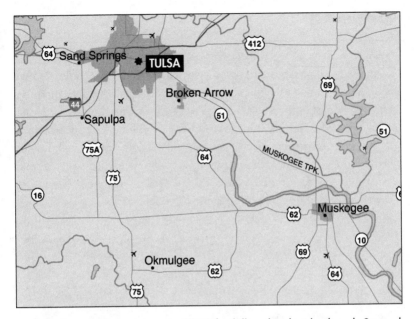

Doss drew a life sentence in 1955 for killing her last husband, Samuel Doss, in Tulsa, with enough arsenic to kill twenty men, according to the coroner. She served 10 years before succumbing to leukemia at age 60 in 1965.

To the end, she insisted that insurance money was not a motivation for her crimes. Mostly, she told interviewers such as *Life* magazine, her husbands bored her. Killing her husbands was part of her search for the ideal husband and permanent wedded bliss.

"I was searching for the perfect mate, the real romance of life."

The press dubbed her the "Giggling Grandma" because she laughed and smiled while confessing to the murders of her husbands.

THE SCENE:

Nanny Doss's Last Home
Oklahoma State Penitentiary
Corner of West and Stonewall Streets
P.O. Box 97
McAlester, OK 74502
918-423-4700

Oregon

Despite its innocuous nickname, the Beaver State has produced an impressive number of high-profile crimes and criminals, including ice-skating medalist and assault conspirator Tonya Harding; Jimmy Rode, the serial killer who got his start from Ted Bundy (Bundy introduced him to personal ads as a source for victims while they were both in jail); Dayton Leroy Rogers, a respectable businessman who was also "The Molalla Forest Killer"; and Randall Woodfield, "I-5 Killer," a former Green Bay Packer who went from exposing himself in public to serial murder.

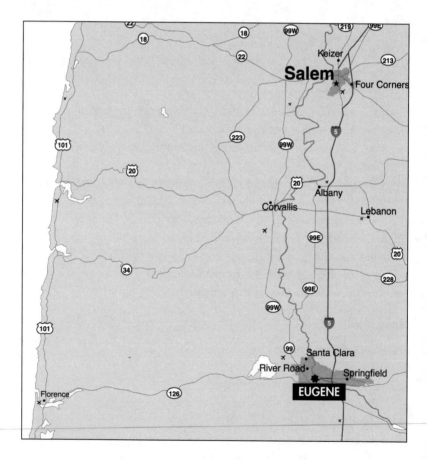

EUGENE

THE STORY: *"Mother Murders Kids for Romance"—1983*

"Call the cops! He shot my kids!" In May 1983, Elizabeth Diane Downs, 28, pulled up to a local hospital emergency room, frantically honking her horn and yelling for help. She told hospital staff and police that a "shaggy-haired stranger" had stopped her car on a deserted country road and shot all three of her children, killing her seven-year-old daughter, Cheryl Lynn, and seriously wounding Christie, eight, and Danny, three.

It was quickly learned that Downs' shaggy stranger was a variation on the old bushy-haired stranger criminals traditionally blame their crimes on to appear innocent. (In the 1950s case of Dr. Sam Sheppard, which inspired *The Fugitive,* it really was a bushy-haired stranger who committed the murder.) In fact, Downs shot her children in order to clear the way for a married lover who wasn't interested in kids. She is now serving a life sentence for murder. Ironically, Downs was a professional surrogate mother who bore children for infertile couples. A TV-movie based on the Ann Rule best-seller, *Small Sacrifices,* was made with Farrah Fawcett in the title role.

THE SCENE:

Cheryl Lynn Downs Murder Scene
Old Mohawk Road and Hill Road
Outside of Springfield, OR

Calling All Cars! Museum Alert!

Police Bureau Museum
16th Floor, Justice Center
1111 SW 2nd Avenue
Portland, OR
503-823-0019

A century of Portland law enforcement history is under arrest here. Badges, historic uniforms, police and criminal weapons, and more. There is also a memorial to human and canine officers slain in the line of duty.

Pennsylvania

Voltaire once observed that if you try something sexually exotic once, you're a philosopher. Do it twice and you're a pervert. Do it three times—or more—in Philadelphia, and you're Gary Heidnik.

Maybe it was the water.

COMFORT FOOD?

In the early afternoon on the day of execution, the state of Pennsylvania lets its condemned choose their last meal. They can select any of the items on the Phase III Final Meal Menu, which features:

37 entrees, from grilled beefsteak to ravioli (but no fettuccine Alfredo). Corned beef is available, but without the cabbage. You can order sauerkraut or cole slaw, though.

13 different preparations of potato

16 soups

22 vegetables

15 salads

12 desserts

8 beverages

ERIE

THE STORY: "Smelly Swag Gives Burglar Away"—1999

 Something smelled funny to the dancers at an Erie strip club—and it wasn't the club. Despite the cigarette smoke, spilled drinks, sweat, and cheap perfume, they noticed that the money they were being tipped with had an unusually strong musty odor.

That led police to arrest a big-tipping club patron who had reportedly stolen $500,000 from a safe at his ex-fiancé's parents' house. The money had been in the tightly-sealed vault for so long, it acquired a potent, mildewed pungence.

The case is pending as of this writing.

THE SCENE:

Kandies Dinner Theater
1402 State Street
Erie, PA 16501-1903
814-454-7304

PHILADELPHIA

THE STORY: *"1960s Guru Accused of Trunk Murder, Flees Country"—1979*

 Ira Einhorn was well known in Philadelphia, where he'd been an outspoken antiwar campaigner and activist in the 1960s. He even ran for mayor once.

In 1977 he was charged with the murder of his missing live-in girlfriend, Helen "Holly" Maddux. Einhorn denied killing her, claiming that she had gone to the food co-op and never returned. Shortly before the trial, Einhorn told a friend, "I'm not going to be able to be Ira Einhorn now," and he fled the country, settling in France.

During a search of Einhorn's apartment on March 28, 1979, detectives found the shriveled body of Maddux stuffed in a steamer trunk in a locked closet. Her body, desiccated by time, weighed only 37 pounds, but it told

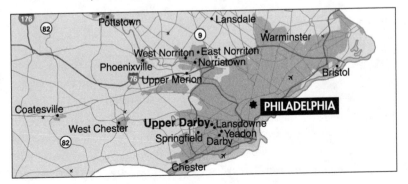

the story of her murder: an angry, blunt force had fractured her skull in six or more places.

Eventually, Einhorn was tried in absentia and convicted. The evidence included: (1) testimony from two friends that he'd asked to help him dispose of the trunk, (2) the students living below his apartment who remembered hearing a scream and a thud, then a year and a half later reported putrid, sticky brown fluid oozing through the ceiling—Einhorn adamantly refused to allow a plumber into his apartment to repair the problem, (3) the testimony of two former girlfriends who'd required hospitalization after trying to break off relationships with Einhorn. One was nearly strangled; the other had a Coke bottle smashed over her head.

Twenty years later he was found living in France, where he was arrested. The French courts refused to extradite him, citing legal "technicalities." In February 1999, the French courts finally agreed to the extradition—except they released him while his appeal was pending (insert the French equivalent of a half-hearted "oops!" here). Maddux family members expect Einhorn to flee again. As of this writing, Einhorn has not returned to the United States to face the 1977 charges.

He did make a declaration of his innocence on the syndicated radio talk show "Radio America" in July 1999, however. "I am innocent of the crime as charged, and I will declare that until my dying breath."

THE SCENE:

Ira Einhorn's Apartment
3411 Race Street, 2nd Floor
Philadelphia, PA

* * * * * *

THE STORY: *"Madman Holds Harem of Sex Slaves"*—1986

 It was a torture dungeon. In the four months before 26-year-old Josephina Rivera managed to escape from the basement of convicted rapist-kidnapper Gary Heidnik's house on Thanksgiving Day 1986, she'd witnessed the arrival and torture of five other women. Two had been murdered. Three were prostitutes; all were black. Heidnik is white.

The Fiend of Franklinville, as he was dubbed by the press, was a former mental patient who had been released after being convicted of kidnapping and raping several retarded black women.

An advanced financial whiz after the time he'd spent in various mental hospitals and prisons, Heidnik was an expert in "stocks and bondage" who invested his way into a fortune, purchasing **the house where his victims were found** and a fleet of expensive cars, including a Rolls-Royce. He sheltered his income by founding his own tax-exempt church and appointing himself bishop.

In 1986, Heidnik began kidnapping women, planning to assemble a harem of ten and create his own tribe. Once inside the house, the women were chained to pipes in the basement and forced to watch while Heidnik raped and tortured the other captives. He shoved screwdrivers in his prisoners' ears and told them, "We'll be just one big happy family." He also turned his live captives into unwitting cannibals by feeding them meals made from prisoners who had died.

At first, Heidnik claimed that the women were already there when he moved in. Later, defense attorneys claimed that Heidnik had been the subject of secret military LSD experiments during the 1960s. Nonetheless, he was quickly convicted of double murder on July 1, 1988. Two days later, he was sentenced to die. He was executed by lethal injection on July 7, 1999.

A punk rock group called Serial Killers recorded "Heidnik's House of Horrors" for the Suspiria label. The album was pressed on blood-red vinyl. Lyrics include, "He had a basement straight out of hell/Marquis de Sade would think it was swell."

THE SCENES:

Gary Heidnik's House
3520 North Marshall Street
   (near Tioga)
Franklinville, PA

Sites where Heidnik found
   several victims:
McDonald's
3800 block of Walnut Street
Philadelphia, PA

Roy Rogers
3800 block of Chestnut Street
(Probably not a Roy Rogers anymore.
   Look for a fast food restaurant.)
Philadelphia, PA

Rhode Island

The smallest state in the Union, "Little Rhody," as the Ocean State is also known, was big enough to host one of the trials of the century in the 1980s: the trial of Claus von Bulow.

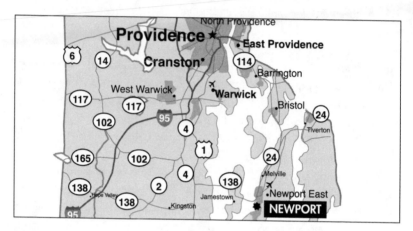

NEWPORT

THE STORY: *"Von Bulow Retried For Murder of Wife"—1982*

It could have been a classic Greek tragedy or a really tawdry soap opera episode—except it was real life. Real life, that is, of the fabulously wealthy.

Claus von Bulow had been convicted in 1979 of murdering his multimillionaire wife Martha "Sunny" von Bulow by injecting her with insulin and causing an irreversible coma so he could marry his mistress and inherit Sunny's millions.

In 1982, in a dramatic retrial after a successful appeal, the defense team proved that Sunny's coma was induced by barbiturates and alcohol and complicated by hypothermia from the length of time spent unconscious on a cold bathroom floor at **the couple's home in Newport**, and Claus was acquitted.

Today, Sunny von Bulow is still alive and comatose in New York City's

Columbia-Presbyterian Hospital. She receives around-the-clock attention from attendants who see to her hair, makeup, and nails in addition to checking her vital signs. A small stereo plays her favorite music.

In honor of her condition, Sunny's children by a previous marriage, the von Auerspergs, have established the Sunny von Bulow Coma and Brain Trauma Foundation in New York.

THE SCENES:

The von Bulows' House
Clarendon Court
Bellevue Avenue at
   Rovensky Avenue,
across from Rovensky Park.
Newport, RI

Columbia-Presbyterian Hospital
622 West 168th Street
New York, NY

South Carolina

The Palmetto State is anything but a crime leader. In 1997, the state's number one crime was not murder, grand larceny, car theft, or domestic violence. It was—drumroll, please—check fraud.

However, what the state lacks in quantity, it more than makes up for in heinous quality.

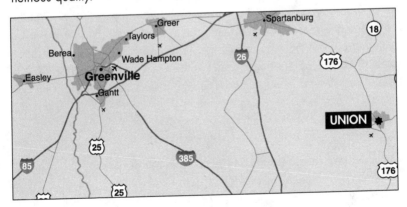

UNION

THE STORY: *"Mother Drowns Her Children To Be with Boyfriend"—1994*

 It was a national obsession. On October 25, 1994, a sobbing small-town South Carolina mother appeared on TV to plead with the mysterious black carjacker who'd taken her little boys, three-year-old Michael and 14-month-old Alexander.

The nation empathized with Susan Smith, 24. Police, state troopers, FBI agents, and thousands of volunteers combed the 515-square-mile county, searching for the car, the kids, or any clue at all. State police set up roadblocks and questioned any man seen with small boys in his car.

While the search was going on, a Florida waitress who had claimed her seven-year-old daughter had been taken from a flea market three days before Smith's boys vanished confessed that she'd hidden her daughter's corpse after her husband had beaten the girl to death. The very next day, a California woman was charged with stabbing her three children—ages four to nine—to death.

The culmination of this wave of infanticide occurred when Susan Smith confessed that there was no carjacker. She'd strapped her boys into their car seats, put up the windows, and let her car roll into **John D. Long Lake** outside Union and watched as it slowly floated out into the lake, filled with water, then flipped over and sank below the surface.

At the trial in Union, Smith's lawyers succeeded in portraying Smith as a victim who'd been abused by her stepfather and divorced by her husband. Smith's attorneys went on to claim that prior to the murders, Smith had been seduced and abandoned by her lover—her boss at the town's textile plant—who'd written her a note saying he wanted to be with her but that he wasn't ready for the responsibilities of a ready-made family. Moved by the tragic portrait, the court spared Smith's life. The death penalty was avoided. She is serving a life sentence without the possibility of parole.

THE SCENE:

John D. Long Lake, Michael and Alex Smith Murder Scene
(There is a permanent memorial.)
Union, SC

South Dakota

The Coyote State is right behind North Dakota when it comes to heinous crime—there isn't much.

A desperate gambler once donned a mask and tried to rob his favorite casino. Things were going smoothly until the teller he was robbing recognized his cologne and addressed him by name. When the teller told the would-be robber the joke wasn't funny, he removed the mask and played a few coins into a slot machine before he wandered out. They took the robbery attempt seriously the next day after casino management discovered that the phone lines had been cut.

The fragrant master criminal got a sentence that was nothing to sniff at: seven years in the state penitentiary.

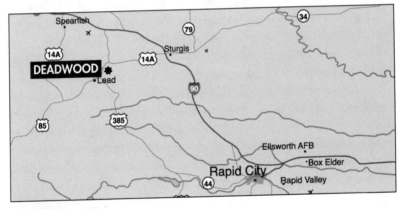

DEADWOOD

THE STORY: *"Wild Bill Hickok Dies in Card Game, Invents Dead Man's Hand"*—1876

 In his life as a lawman, James Butler "Wild Bill" Hickok had more than his fair share of lucky breaks. On July 17, 1870, when he was the sheriff of Hays City, Kansas, Hickok was overpowered by seven intoxicated cavalry troopers who held him down while one of them stuck a six-gun in his ear and pulled the trigger—the gun misfired. Hickok got to his feet and shot several of the troopers and the rest fled.

When his career as a lawman ended, Hickok toured with his friend William Frederick "Buffalo Bill" Cody's Wild West show. After that, he mostly hung around Deadwood, playing cards and drinking.

On August 1, 1876, Jack McCall, a laborer, lost all his money, $110, to Hickok in a card game. Even though Hickok gave McCall breakfast money, McCall swore revenge.

The next day, Hickok was playing cards at **Saloon Number 10**. Uncharacteristically, he sat facing the door, with his back to the room, instead of taking his usual seat against the wall. McCall wandered into the bar, ordered a drink and slowly walked up behind Hickok and fired a single shot into his back. Hickok fell to the floor, dead, still clutching his poker hand. The hand, a pair of black aces and a pair of black eights, has been known as "The Dead Man's Hand" ever since.

The bullet that killed Hickok went through his body and lodged in another card player's wrist. The gambler, William Rodney Massie, never had it removed and it was there when he died in 1910.

After several trials, McCall went to the gallows on March 1, 1877. He was buried in an unmarked grave.

In a postscript to the story, Calamity Jane (the Wild West character who looked nothing like Doris Day, who played her in movies) died in Terry on August 1, 1903, not far from Deadwood. For years, she'd claimed to have been Hickok's sweetheart, which he'd always denied. Per her dying wish, she was buried next to him. Hickok, who considered Calamity Jane a nuisance when they were alive, lies next to her forever.

THE SCENES:

Saloon Number 10
657 Main Street
Deadwood, SD
800-952-9398

Wild Bill Hickok's Tombstone
Mount Moriah Cemetery
10 Mount Moriah
Deadwood, SD

You can view a photo of **Hickok's tombstone** on the World Wide Web at www.policeguide.com/cemetery.htm

Tennessee

Tennessee has often been considered three states in one. East Tennessee, with the Great Smoky Mountains, has Chattanooga, and Knoxville. Middle Tennessee, between the Cumberland Plateau and the lower Tennessee River, has Nashville, the state capital, and the Grand Ole Opry. West Tennessee is Deep South cotton country, with Memphis, the capital of the Mississippi Delta region. But when it comes to crime scenes, the state has a single history: interesting.

From the capture of George "Machine Gun" Kelly to the setting for John Grisham's modern thriller, *The Firm*, the Volunteer State's motto, "agriculture and commerce" should include fascinating crime.

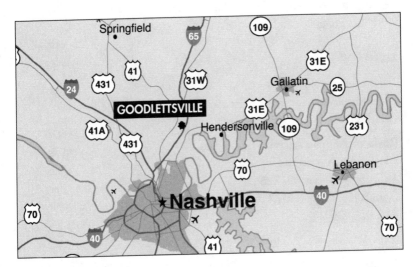

GOODLETTSVILLE

THE STORY: "Hee Haw *Star and Wife Robbed, Murdered*"—1973

Grandpa Jones and David "Stringbean" Akeman, best friends, had been performing together at the Grand Ole Opry and on *Hee Haw* for decades. The two were so close that they alternated sitting and talking in front of their shared neighboring properties, just north of Nashville, each day.

After performing at the Opry on November 9, 1973, the two planned to leave the next morning for a hunting trip to Virginia. At 6:40 A.M. on November 10, Jones walked over to get Akeman and found the body of Akeman's wife, Estelle, dead in the front yard, where she'd been shot. He found Akeman inside the house, beaten and shot to death. The house had been ransacked.

A year later, cousins John and Douglas Brown were arrested after bragging about committing the murders when trying to rob Akeman of the fortune in cash he reportedly kept on the farm because he didn't trust banks. Akeman refused to tell them where he'd hidden the money, so they killed him and his wife. The two were convicted and sent to prison.

In 1996, a man renting the farm found Akeman's money behind a stone in the fireplace mantel. Unfortunately, mice had shredded it into worthless confetti.

THE SCENES:

The Akemans' House
On Baker Road near the intersection at Baker Station Road
Goodlettsville, TN

David and Estelle Akeman Grave Site
Forest Lawn Memorial Gardens
1150 South Dickerson Road
Goodlettsville, TN 37022
615-859-5279

MEMPHIS

THE STORY: *"Civil Rights Pioneer Killed Outside Hotel Room"*—1968

He had a dream. But Dr. Martin Luther King's dream of racial harmony ended on the night of April 4, 1968, as he stepped on the balcony outside his room **(#306) at Lorraine Motel** in downtown Memphis to ask aides if he'd need a coat.

King was leaving for a dinner. Jesse Jackson, Andrew Young, an aide named James Orange, and Dr. King's driver were waiting by the car at the foot of the stairs.

He stepped out of the room and into the rifle scope of a sniper across the street. The single shot was fired from the common bathroom window of a small rooming house directly across the street.

James Earl Ray, a recently released convict, was quickly arrested. The string of evidence seemed ironclad. Ray had rented a room at the rooming house under an alias and purchased a rifle with a scope six days before the shooting. He was convicted directly and received a 99-year sentence.

Despite this, to his dying day on April 23, 1998, Ray maintained that he was framed. Investigators and the King family now believe that Ray was innocent. They've asked that the case be reopened so that sophisticated tests can be conducted on Ray's rifle and the bullet that killed Dr. King to resolve lingering doubts. At press time, no new information has been found.

The hotel was converted into the National Civil Rights Museum in 1991 to honor Dr. King's legacy and the entire Civil Rights movement.

THE SCENE:

Lorraine Motel (now National Civil Rights Museum)
450 Mulberry St.
Memphis, TN
901-521-9699

* * * * * *

THE STORY: *"Girlfriend Attacks Singer with Hot Grits, Kills Self"—1974*

 At 4:00 A.M. on October 18, 1974, soul-singing superstar Al Green, age 27, and two female houseguests had just returned to his home after a recording session.

Green, best known for chart-busting hits "Let's Stay Together" and "I'm Still in Love with You," went upstairs to take a bath. A few minutes later one of the two women, Mary Woodson, age 28, later identified as Green's girlfriend, barged into the bathroom and hurled a pot of boiling grits on Green, burning him severely on the back, abdomen, and arm as he tried to get out of the tub. Then she ran into the adjacent bedroom and, after several attempts, shot herself in the head.

According to police, who confirmed the death a suicide, two of the bullets were found in a wall and a couch, the last one in Ms. Woodson. The shots came from a .38-caliber pistol registered to Green. The other woman, Carlotta Williams, 21, told police she was in another bedroom during the assault and shooting.

Green told police he had no idea what caused the attack.

Detectives found a three-page suicide note in Woodson's purse. She'd also mailed a copy of the letter to Green's office. It arrived a week after the attack.

Believing the incident was a sign from God, Green became an ordained pastor of the **Full Gospel Tabernacle** and started a ministry. After narrowly escaping serious injury falling off a Cincinnati stage in 1979, Green decided he'd had another divine hint and returned to his gospel music roots exclusively. He didn't record another R&B song until 1988 when he sang "Put a Little Love in Your Heart" with Annie Lennox for the Bill Murray film *Scrooged*.

THE SCENE:

Full Gospel Tabernacle Church
787 Hale Road
Memphis, TN 38116
901-794-6220

Calling All Cars! Museum Alert!

Memphis Police Department Museum
Beale Street Police Station
159 Beale Street
Memphis, TN 38103
901-525-9800

Weapons, displays of Memphis area crimes of the past, and other highlights from the history of one of the nation's most innovative police departments are featured here. Located in a working police substation, the museum is open 24 hours a day.

Texas

Welcome to the gunfighter state.

No state has a closer relationship with guns and crime than Texas. Texas plus firearms is an equation that has changed state, national, and world history ever since Samuel Colt began mass-producing "The Great Equalizers."

The Lone Star State practically invented "the lone gunman."

In addition to peculiar gun laws, the state also has some very creative lawmakers. In 1999, Texas state Rep. John Longoria of San Antonio planned to introduce legislation making it illegal for teenagers to "make out." Some have wondered if Longoria might have a daughter who's approaching sweet sixteen.

AUSTIN

THE STORY: *"Texas Tower Sniper Kills 16"—1966*

 At 11:48 A.M. on August 1, 1966, in the days before SWAT teams or any organized paramilitary emergency response programs existed—even before personal walkie-talkies were standard equipment for police officers, Charles Whitman, 25, a mentally disturbed ex-Marine and, in his time, one of the youngest Eagle scouts in the country, went to the top of the **University of Texas Tower** armed for a small war and began shooting pedestrians below.

In the next 90 minutes on that hot summer day, he killed 16 people and wounded another 31 before being killed by police. The heroes of the day were the two police officers who stopped Whitman: Houston McCoy and Ramiro Martinez. The school landmark stayed open until 1975, when it was closed after a string of students committed suicide by leaping off the tower. It was reopened to the public in the spring of 1999. The open-air observation deck atop the 231-foot tower has had security bars installed to prevent suicides or homicides.

A single bullet pockmark near the base of the **Jefferson Davis statue** is the only remaining sign of the 1966 shooting. Thirty years later, the

Austin *American-Statesman* reported that an actor who starred in a film based on the incident, who bears an uncanny physical resemblance to Whitman, was hit by a stray bullet on a street near the tower in March on his first visit to Austin (reported in "News of The Weird," 09-12-1996).

THE SCENE:

University of Texas Tower
Off 24th between Guadalupe and Speedway
Austin, TX

Calling All Cars! Museum Alert!

Texas State Prison Museum
1113 12th St.
Huntsville, TX
409-295-2155

See "Old Sparky," the Lone Star of Texas justice, an electric chair built by inmates. From 1924 to 1964, it outlived 361 condemned men. Also built by inmates, see the display of makeshift weapons and Clyde Barrow's rifle.

DALLAS

TOMB IT MAY CONCERN

After deputies ended their crime spree, Bonnie and Clyde (and Clyde's brother Buck) were buried back in Texas, perhaps the only state big enough to hold their legend (see Gibsland, Louisiana).

Clyde Barrow and Buck Barrow
Western Heights Cemetery
Dallas, Texas
1617 Fort Worth Avenue
Dallas, TX

Bonnie Parker
Crown Hill Memorial Park
9700 Webb Chapel Road
Dallas, TX

THE STORY: *"President Kennedy Assassinated. Who (and How Many) Dunit?"—1963*

November 22, 1963. A popular president is assassinated. Afterward, numerous phrases became part of the cultural consciousness. A grassy knoll. The Umbrella Man. The Zapruder film. Anyone who was around then can tell you where they were and what they were doing. The suspected killer, Lee Harvey Oswald, is murdered (on TV) days after the shooting and long before a trial can be held.

Reports issued by various government agencies and fact-finding groups only add to the confusion. In 1964, the FBI said it was One Shooter, Three Shots—Three Hits. Later that same year, the Warren Commission (which included Senator Arlen "Lone Bullet" Specter) concluded that it was One Shooter, Three Shots—Two Hits and One Miss. However, in 1979, the House Select Committee on Assassinations decided that it was At Least Two Shooters, At Least Four Shots, At Least Two Misses.

Former New Orleans District Attorney Jim Garrison, Oliver Stone, and thousands of others say Oswald definitely couldn't have done it alone—if he did it at all.

There are only three certainties. (1) The Lone Nut with a Gun concept was practically invented in Texas. It was certainly perfected here. (2) The nation lost a beloved president. (3) Here's your chance to take a look for yourself.

THE SCENE:

The Sixth Floor Museum
Texas School Book Depository
411 Elm Street (at Houston Street)
Dallas, TX 72020
888-485-4854

The sniper's perch Lee Harvey Oswald is said to have shot President Kennedy from has been turned into a museum. See how it looked the day the president was killed.

Scope It Out for Yourself!

You don't have to go to Dallas to get an alleged assassin's eye view of the killing ground. The Sixth Floor Museum has added a very unique exhibit: Earthcam's Dealey Plaza Cam. You can peer out the window of the Texas School Book Depository and see frequently updated live images of the plaza. For complete realism, feel free to draw your own crosshairs on your computer monitor. Go to www.jfk.org.

Calling All Cars! Museum Alert!

The Conspiracy Museum
110 South Market Street
Dallas, TX 75202
214-741-3040

Around the corner from the book depository, "assassinologist" R.B. Cutler, a Harvard-educated architect, gives personal tours of the Kennedy assassination scene. His museum also traces the history of American assassinations back to Andrew Jackson.

TOMB IT MAY CONCERN

Lee Harvey Oswald
Rose Hill Memorial Park
7301 East Lancaster
Fort Worth, Texas

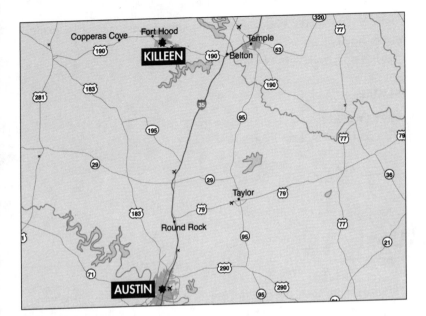

KILLEEN

THE STORY: *"Gunman Kills 23, Wounds 27 in Cafeteria Massacre"*—1991

 October 16, 1991 was National Bosses' Day. **Luby's Cafeteria** was a crowded, happy place. At lunchtime, with 150 people having lunch and socializing, George "Jo-Jo" Hennard, Jr. crashed his blue 1987 Ford Ranger pickup truck through Luby's plate-glass front window and began firing both of his 9mm semiautomatic pistols almost immediately afterward. He stalked through the restaurant, methodically choosing his victims, mostly women, shouting, "All women of Killeen and Belton are vipers! See what you've done to me and my family!"

Calmly reloading and firing single shots into the heads of his victims at point-blank range, he yelled, "Is it worth it? Tell me, is it worth it?"

By the time police arrived, Hennard had killed 22 in the restaurant, one more died later, and 27 others were wounded.

Hennard received four wounds in the shootout with police before running into the restroom and using the final bullet in his magazine to shoot himself in the head.

In only 10 minutes it had become the largest mass murder by gunfire in U.S. history.

To this day, no one knows what set Hennard off.

THE SCENE:

Luby's Cafeteria
1705 East Central Texas Expressway
Killeen, TX
254-628-8500

Utah

It takes more than bees to get the Beehive State buzzing. The state's rugged terrain produced such rugged individualists as Robert Leroy Parker (Butch Cassidy, born in Beaver) and the craggy mountains of Arches National Park were the backdrop for feminist anthem *Thelma and Louise*.

Postscript: it's a little-known fact that the residents of Salt Lake City eat more lime Jell-O than any other place in the world, which could be one possible explanation.

OREM

THE STORY: "Ex-con Goes on Murder Spree,
 Demands Right To Be Executed"—1977

On July 19, 1976, just three months after being released from his latest prison term, career criminal Gary Gilmore went on a robbery/killing spree that resulted in the deaths of a 24-year-old service station attendant in Orem and, the next night, a motel manager. Both victims were shot in the head after complying with orders to lie down.

After his capture and conviction, Gilmore refused to fight the execution order, demanding to be killed by a firing squad, a right in Utah. Gilmore became a media sensation after he attempted suicide twice and went on

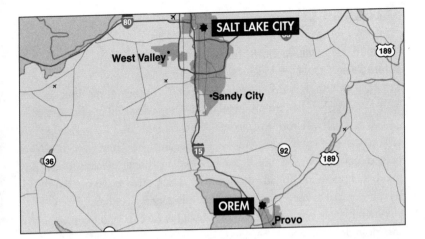

a 25-day hunger strike during his two-and-a-half-month death watch. He also refused help from the American Civil Liberties Union and waived his right to appeal to the U.S. Supreme Court.

Just after 8 A.M. on January 17, 1977, Gilmore was strapped into a wooden chair in front of a wall of mattresses, plywood, and sandbags. A hood was placed over his head and a paper target was pinned on his chest. Thirty feet away, five marksmen trained their rifles on the target through holes in a canvas sheet and waited for the order to shoot. To relieve the executioners of any guilt from firing the fatal shot, one of the rifles contained a blank. No one knows which one.

When asked if he had any last words, Gilmore shook his head and simply said, "Let's do it." Moments later, they did.

At the time, it was the first execution of any kind in the United States in ten years.

Norman Mailer's best-selling book *Executioner's Song* was later made into a TV mini-series starring Tommy Lee Jones and Rosanna Arquette.

THE SCENES:

Sinclair Gas Station
168 East and 800 North
Orem, UT

City Center Inn
150 West, 300 South
Provo, UT
801-373-8489

SALT LAKE CITY

THE STORY: *"Mormon Document Forger Kills Two Before Being Caught"—1985*

 Mark Hofmann was a respected member of the Mormon community who fancied himself a dealer in rare documents. He'd earned over $2 million dollars selling the extremely rare Mormon documents he "discovered." What he'd discovered was a classic scam. Mormon church officials would pay exorbitant prices for "found" documents that purported to expose the church as a hoax, just to keep them away from critics and historians.

When people became suspicious about his success and unusual behavior, Hofmann became a murderer. On October 15, 1985, he used pipe bombs to kill his business partners, Steven Christensen and Kathleen Sheets, and divert attention away from him. The plan might have worked if he hadn't severely injured himself on October 16 when one of his bombs exploded prematurely. Though Hofmann later claimed it was a failed suicide attempt, police believe he was en route to blow up another victim when the bomb went off.

Several books have been written about the case and a film was in development. But a four-hour miniseries, *The Mormon Murders*, was postponed indefinitely. Sources have hinted that the cancellation was the result of the Mormon Church's influence.

THE SCENES:

Steven Christensen Murder Site
The Judge Building
300 South and Main streets
Salt Lake City, UT

Kathleen Sheets Murder Site
4630 Naniola Drive
Salt Lake City, UT

Hofmann's Premature Explosion Site
200 North (between West Temple and
    Main streets)
(5 minutes away from the
    Mormon Temple)
Salt Lake City, UT

Vermont

There are so few murders here in the Green Mountain State, which had the second lowest homicide rate in the nation in 1994, Vermont has had to import its murderers.

WEST DOVER

THE STORY: "Long Island Man Claims Painters Molested and Killed His Wife"—1994

Things were not looking good for Long Island, New York resident John Grega in the summer of 1994. His wife of eight years had given him one last chance to permanently quit drinking and cocaine or else she'd leave him. And he'd fallen off the wagon. And, as he told his friends, his wife had stopped having sex with him.

While they tried to work things out, the family borrowed a friend's Vermont condominium. On the morning of September 12, they took their 2-year-old son to "Santa's Land" amusement park in Putney and arrived back at the condo around midday.

According to Grega, he took their son out to a playground for the afternoon to give his wife, Christine, 31, some peace and quiet. When he came home at sunset, he found his wife dead in the bathtub. According to police, his claim that painters working on the house had killed his wife was a suspicious story from the start. They found Christine Grega lying in a puddle of water on the bathroom floor next to a Jacuzzi. Her upper body was bruised and swelling, preventing paramedics from inserting a breathing tube in her throat.

Medical examiners later found evidence that Christine had been strangled and sodomized so severely that she'd have required stitches if she had survived. Christine also sustained severe head injuries.

Confronted with the evidence, Grega admitted to having what he described as "consensual" anal sex with his wife on the afternoon of her death and allowed that he may have had his hands around her neck during rough sex, but that she was fine when he left with their son.

Police were unable to find any witnesses who were at the playground between 5 and 6:30 P.M. and saw anyone matching Grega's description, or the red Volkswagen the family owned. They also discovered that Grega had two insurance polices on his wife valued at a combined $150,000. At the trial, Grega claimed that house painters who were working in the apartment complex at the time had broken in and committed the crime.

The Vermont jury didn't buy Grega's story and on August 4, 1995, he was convicted of aggravated murder and aggravated sexual assault in the death of his wife and given a mandatory life sentence without parole. Grega is appealing the conviction.

THE SCENE:

Timber Creek Condominiums
Unit 94
Route 100 North
West Dover, VT

WHODUNIT HOTEL

The North Hero House
P.O. Box 155
North Hero, VT 05474
888-525-3644

Experience a night of thrills, chills, and lots of fun as The North Hero House and Beaner Productions bring you "Death is a Cabaret" murder mystery.

The North Hero House Country Inn and Restaurant is a historic bed and breakfast located in the Lake Champlain Islands of northern Vermont with a spectacular view of the Green Mountains and Mount Mansfield. The 26-room inn was built in 1891, when guests arrived by steamship. The inn was beautifully restored in 1997, with antiques and modern conveniences required by today's travelers.

Virginia

You've got to wonder about a state whose motto *Sic Semper Tyrannis* (Thus Shall It Ever Be for Tyrants!) is the very same phrase triumphantly uttered by John Wilkes Booth after he shot President Lincoln.

Nonetheless, criminals are dying to get out of Virginia. Literally.

The twelfth largest state in population, Virginia led the nation in 1996 with eight executions. Virginia also invented "lynching," only in those days, it meant a whipping, not a hanging.

There are still plenty of crime scenes to ogle. Which is why crime scene fans will be singing, "Carry Me Back to Old Virginia."

It Would Be a Crime if You Missed . . .

The Birthplace of Lynching
Historic Marker (which reads: "ORIGIN OF LYNCH LAW")
Route 29, one mile north of Altavista
Altavista, VA

In 1780, Colonel Charles Lynch and others whipped British-sympathizing Tories and other criminals after a perfunctory trial, which formed the basis for "Lynch" laws. The term "lynching" evolved to describe punishments meted out by angry mobs, including tarring and feathering, and hanging.

ARLINGTON

THE STORY: *"Most Notorious and Destructive Spy in CIA History Arrested"—1994*

Aldrich Hazen Ames, 52, a 31-year CIA veteran and former branch chief of counterintelligence in the Soviet division of the Operations Directorate, and his Colombian-born wife, Maria del Rosario Casas Ames, 41, were arrested on February 21, 1994, at their home for leaking information on almost all top-secret U.S. operations in the Soviet Union to the KGB.

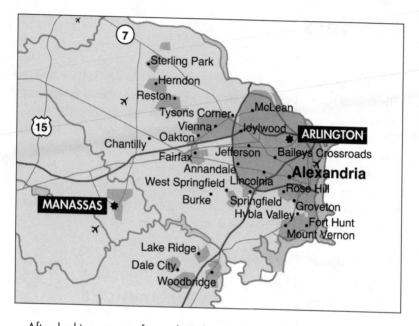

After leaking secrets for a decade, Ames got careless. In addition to living well above his means, he neglected to destroy incriminating evidence. In a daring late-night caper, FBI agents stole Ames' trash and found a ripped up Post-it note with plans for a meeting between Ames and his Russian handlers in Bogota, Colombia. A few days later, they followed Ames in the early morning hours as he put a horizontal chalk mark on **a mailbox in northwest Washington** to let the Russians know he was confirming the Colombia trip. The mailbox was chosen because Russian personnel routinely passed it en route to the embassy.

Under a plea bargain, Aldrich Ames is serving a life sentence and Maria Ames received 63 months, the minimum sentence. With time served and good behavior, she could be released in 2000.

THE SCENES:

The Ames' House
2512 North Randolph Street
Arlington, VA

Ames' Handler's Contact Site
mailbox at the corner of 37th
    and R Streets
Washington, DC

MANASSAS

THE STORY: *"Surgeons Attach Man's Severed Penis"—1993*

 After the latest argument and beating, ex-Marine John Wayne Bobbitt's wife, Lorena, had had enough. She took a kitchen knife and sliced her sleeping husband's penis off and fled the house as he howled in pain. When police gave chase, she waved the severed member out of her car window and tossed it in a field.

Bobbitt and his penis were both rushed to Prince William Hospital, where they were reconnected.

In 1994, a jury of five men and seven women acquitted Lorena of malicious wounding on the grounds of temporary insanity.

John Bobbitt and his penis later performed a stand-up act at comedy clubs across the country and starred in a porno movie. In 1994, the ex-Marine starred in a hard-core, X-rated video, *John Wayne Bobbitt Uncut.*

THE SCENE:

The Bobbitts' House
Maplewood drive off Centreville Road (route 28).
It's the apartment complex across the street from the Maplewood Plaza shopping center in Manassas, VA.

Washington

As the state that hosts many league-leading serial killers, both captured and uncaptured, and the reigning monarchy of true crime writers, it is no surprise that Washington is also the home state of Starbucks and the ultra-caffeinated espresso movement: everyone's afraid to fall asleep.

It's hard to picture slumber here, since state residents have made some fairly eye-opening contributions to the annals of crime, including lust killer Ted Bundy (over 22 *known* victims; born in Vermont, he moved west at an early age); the at-large Green River Killer (who murdered 49 women between 1982–1984); the at-large Green River Copycat Killer in Spokane (eight women between 1996–1997); the at-large Northwest Serial Killer (42 victims since 1985); and Keith Jesperson, the "Happy Face Killer" (an interstate trucker who killed eight women in the 1990s and doodled happy faces on the letters he sent to the press boasting about his crimes).

OLYMPIA

THE STORY: *"'Hollywood' Bank Robbery Gang Had Treehouse Hideout"—1996*

It's a story that closely imitates the 1991 movie *Point Break,* about a bank-robbing gang of surfing thrill-seekers led by Patrick Swayze. Profiled in Ann Rule's best-selling *The End of The Dream: The Golden Boy Who Never Grew Up,* William Scott Scurlock was a charming, charismatic free-spirited athlete and preacher's son who led a gang of professional bank robbers. Scurlock lived a high-style life from a **multistory dream treehouse** that had been featured in a number of newspapers and architectural magazines throughout the gang's most active period.

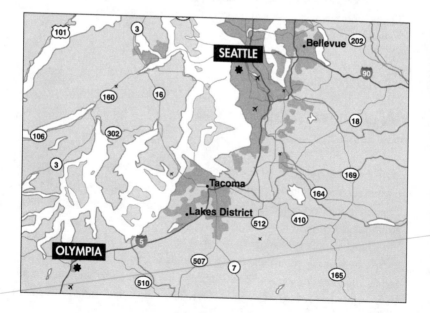

Known as "The Hollywood Bandits" for their intricate disguises, split-second timing, and bold robberies that netted millions, the gang was one of the most notorious in the Puget Sound area and recent criminal history.

Surrounded by police after a robbery on Thanksgiving Day 1996, Scurlock took his own life rather than face capture.

THE SCENE:

William Scott Scurlock's Treehouse
"Seven Cedars" is off Overhulse Road past Evergreen State College in Olympia, WA.

SEATTLE

THE STORY: *"High-school Teacher Has Affair, Then Child, with Student"—1997*

 It's an old crime story. Boy, 13, meets teacher, 36, and they have a child. Teacher is convicted of second-degree child rape, gets suspended sentence, and is ordered to undergo sex-offender treatment and have no further contact with the boy. Naturally, she and the boy are quickly back together and conceive a second child, which she delivers in prison in October 1998.

In this case, the teacher was Mary Kay Letourneau, a married mother of four and daughter of ultraconservative former California Republican Congressman John Schmitz. Letourneau was teaching in the Seattle-area Highline School District when she began a sexual relationship with Vili Fualaau, then 13, who had been her student in the second and sixth grades. Letourneau's first husband has custody of their kids and Fualaau's parents have custody of their son's children with Letourneau.

Fualaau has repeatedly denied being a victim, and his mother and other relatives have said they accept Letourneau as a member of their family. A three-hundred-page book telling the couple's side of the story was released in October 1998 in Europe, titled *Un Seul Crime, L'Amour (Only One Crime, Love)*. It is not available in the United States. Most of the book contains protestations by the couple that their love cannot be outlawed.

THE SCENES:

Vili Fualaau's Alma Mater
Shorewood Elementary School
2725 SW 116th Street
Burien, WA

Mary Kay Letourneau's Current Residence
Purdy Correctional Center
10109 South Tacoma Way
Gig Harbor, WA

Washington, D.C.

Paraphrasing Shakespeare, the gunplay's the thing in the District of Columbia. Like Texas, D.C. is a place where guns are closely intertwined with its history. In addition to numerous shootings in public places and assorted VIP assassination attempts, Watergate burglars were the "smoking guns" that shot down a president.

THE STORY: *"Stalker Shoots President to Impress Actress"—1981*

 While President Reagan was leaving the **Washington Hilton Hotel** after giving a speech, John Warnock Hinckley, Jr. whipped out a .22-caliber pistol and began firing Devastator exploding bullets at the president.

Initially, President Reagan was unaware that he'd been wounded. After removing the president's shirt, they found a bullet lodged an inch away from his heart. The president made a speedy recovery after surgery.

Hinckley, who had stalked actress Jodie Foster while she was a student at Yale University, was convinced that by assassinating the president he could win Foster's "respect and love."

On June 21, 1982, after seven weeks of testimony and three days of jury deliberation, John Hinckley, Jr. was found not guilty by reason of insanity. He currently resides at **St. Elizabeth's Mental Hospital** for an indefinite term.

Washington Hilton Hotel
1919 Connecticut Avenue
Washington, DC
202-483-3000

St. Elizabeth's Mental Hospital
2700 Martin Luther King Avenue SE
Washington, DC

* * * * * *

FORD'S THEATRE—LINCOLN'S LAST OUTING.

THE STORY: *"Actor Shoots President, Flees"—1865*

On the evening of April 14, 1865, Abraham Lincoln, his wife, and two guests watched a performance of *Our American Cousin* from the presidential box at **Ford's Theatre**.

That night, armed with a pistol and a knife, John Wilkes Booth, an actor and fanatical Confederate sympathizer, slipped past Pinkerton bodyguards and fired a shot into Lincoln's head.

In the confusion, Booth slashed the arm of Lincoln's guest with his knife, vaulted over the railing onto the stage, a 12-foot drop, catching a spur from his riding boots in the American flag draped over the railing, and landed awkwardly, breaking a small bone in his left ankle.

An actor to the end, once Booth found himself at center stage, he couldn't resist the chance for a melodramatic gesture. Still clutching his knife, he leaned on his good leg and shouted to the audience, *"Sic Semper Tyrannis!"* ("Thus shall it ever be for tyrants!"), and hobbled across the stage to the wings yelling, "The South is avenged!"

John Ford tried to reopen the theater after Lincoln's death, but arson threats kept the doors closed. The government bought the theater in 1866 and turned it into an office building and later a warehouse and museum. In 1954, President Dwight D. Eisenhower signed a Congressional act to restore the theater. Reconstruction began ten years later, and the newly restored Ford's Theatre opened in 1968 with the play *John Brown's Body*.

The theater has a year-round schedule of productions.

THE SCENE:

Ford's Theatre
511 Tenth Street, NW
Washington, DC
202-638-2941
Fax: 202-638-1001
onstage@fordstheatre.org
www.fordstheatre.org

Calling All Cars! Museum Alert!

FBI Headquarters
935 Pennsylvania Ave NW
Washington, DC
202-737-3759

The most comprehensive collection of American criminal history, law enforcement, murder weapons, and forensic science displays anywhere. One of the highlights of the tour is watching the tour guide, a Special Agent, shoot up a target. Ask nicely and he or she might give you the used target.

The Premier Hotel
(formerly Howard Johnson's)—Watergate Break-in Lookout Site
2601 Virginia Avenue NW
Washington, D.C.
800-965-6869
202-965-2700
www.premierdc.com

On June 17, 1972, a member of the bungling Watergate burglary team used room 723 as a lookout for the break-in at Democratic National Committee headquarters across the street.

From there, the lookout got to watch his five partners in crime get caught by police as they adjusted bugging equipment they had installed during a previous break-in in May and attempted to photograph the Democrats' strategic documents.

You can stay in room 723. It now has lots of memorabilia from the event. Just ask for the Watergate Room.

While you're there, ask about Watergate Liquors. If you're a liquor fan, you'll love breaking into your own bottle of Watergate brand vodka and scotch.

West Virginia

The legend on the state license plates reads "Wild, Wonderful West Virginia." And it certainly is.

One of America's most notorious serial wife-killers, a murdering pastor, and Charles Manson have all called the Mountain State home.

It may be among the smallest states, but it certainly has some of the biggest crime scene thrills.

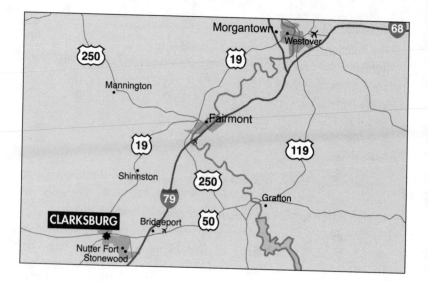

CLARKSBURG

THE STORY: *"American Bluebeard Kills 50-plus 'Wives' in Homemade Gas Chamber"—1930s*

 Used furniture dealer Herman Drenth was a very busy man. Although Drenth was legally married in Clarksburg, police later learned that his frequent "business" trips across the country included bigamy and murder.

Drenth would find wealthy widows from Boston to Spokane through classified ads, marry them, and bring them back to his two-room "**scientific laboratory**" in the woods outside Clarksburg. From the glass window of the "operations" room, he'd watch his bound victim struggle against the poisonous gas he'd pipe into the killing chamber. Drenth would keep their cash and the money he made from selling their property.

Drenth used a hammer to kill the three young children of his last victim just before he gassed her.

After investigating reports about missing women, police followed "Harry Powers," as Drenth was known, from the **Clarksburg post office** to his "lab." The noxious fumes from five corpses rotting in a nearby ditch led police to arrest Drenth, who readily confessed. He also admitted that the sexual pleasure from watching his victims die "beat any cathouse I was ever in."

Ironically, Drenth refused to tell police about his other victims, explaining, "You got me on five. What good would fifty more do?"

Drenth was hanged at Moundsville Penitentiary on March 18, 1932, without ever providing further information.

Many Clarksburg natives still claim to have relatives who were hired by "Powers" to do digging at what is known as "The Murder Farm."

THE SCENES:

Herman Drenth's Murder "Lab" (now Chuck's Upholstery Shop)
Quiet Dell suburb of
   Clarksburg, WV
304-624-9571

Clarksburg Post Office Building
Pike and Third Streets
Clarksburg, WV

"Harry Powers" Residence
111 Quincy Street
Broad Oak suburb of Clarksburg, WV

CLIFFTOP

THE STORY: "Minister Accused of Murdering Wife To Be with Man"—1996

 Responding to a call for help at 2:00 A.M. on April 30, 1996, sheriff's deputies found Cheryl Jewell Flippo, 46, beaten to death at a secluded cabin in **Babcock State Park**. She'd sustained at least seven powerful blows to the head with a heavy, blunt object, possibly a piece of firewood. She also sustained defensive wounds to the arms and hands.

Her husband, Reverend J. Michael Flippo, 49, pastor of the **Landmark Church of God**, claimed that a masked attacker broke in while they were sleeping. Directly after the investigation, Rev. Flippo was arrested for the murder of his wife of 28 years. At the trial, prosecutors cited a lack of evidence supporting the presence of an outside attacker. In addition, there were numerous signs that the crime scene had been staged. In terms of defensive wounds, the scratches Flippo claimed he got in the fight were minimal, while Mrs. Flippo's hands and wrists were broken in the desperate fight for her life.

Evidence suggesting Flippo's guilt began to pour in. Flippo had taken out a $100,000 life insurance policy on Cheryl less than a month before the murder, records indicated that Flippo had run up credit card debts, and evidence showed he embezzled money from the church, including over $15,000 from a child's liver transplant fund.

Soon after the insurance policy was opened, the couple began complaining about a stalker, reporting several murder attempts.

Police suspected that Flippo had been having a close, possibly sexual, relationship with a male parishioner. Prior to the murder, the two men allegedly spent a night together in the same hotel bed, and they'd met in Babcock State Park two days before Flippo booked **Cabin 13**. At the crime scene police found photos of the male parishioner undressing and a letter by Mrs. Flippo complaining about being in competition for her husband's affections. At the trial, the state prosecutor theorized that this extramarital relationship was a catalyst for the murder.

In October 1997, Flippo was convicted and received a life sentence without possibility for parole, but in October 1999 the U.S. Supreme Court reversed the decision by the trial court to allow the photos to be used as evidence in the trial. The case was remanded back to the Fayette county court for a ruling on the evidence consistent with the U.S. Supreme Court's decision. If the court determines that a 911 call does not grant the police permission to search the premises, state's evidence, i.e., the photos, may become inadmissible.

THE SCENES:

Babcock State Park
Cabin 13
Clifftop, WV

Landmark Church of God
1st Avenue and 19th Street
Nitro, WV
304-755-0470

The Flippos' House
1218 West 12th Street
Nitro, WV

Wisconsin

When it comes to serial killers, California is quantity, but Wisconsin is quality.

Where else would you find two all-time league-leading heinous serial monsters like Ed Gein, who inspired at least three classic horror movies, and Jeffrey Dahmer, who ate more people than any known American cannibal since New York's Albert Fish?

Hmm. Jeffrey Dahmer and the state with the highest per-capita incidence of obesity. Coincidence?

MILWAUKEE

THE STORY: *"Former Policewoman, Ex-Playboy Bunny Convicted of Murder"—1981*

 It was a story made-for-TV-movie producers would kill for. Lawrencia "Bambi" Bembenek, a tall, 23-year-old blonde, calendar pinup, former Playboy bunny, and ex-police officer was convicted in the May 1981 murder of her husband's ex-wife. She quickly became America's imprisoned sweetheart in the mid-1980s.

In the fall of 1980, after a whirlwind romance, Bembenek married 32-year-old Milwaukee police detective Elfred "Fred" Schultz—along with the crippling alimony and mortgage payments that claimed half his pay.

When Schultz's ex-wife was shot to death by a mysterious intruder using a .38-caliber pistol, Fred's off-duty weapon, a .38-caliber revolver, was promptly inspected. It hadn't been fired. But investigators failed to record the gun's serial number. Later, when Fred's off-duty "unfired" gun was re-tested for ballistics, the gun matched.

Since Fred was sitting in the police station at the time of the murder, Bembenek was charged with the killing and convicted on a string of circumstantial evidence, including access to the gun and the keys to Christine's house, hair fiber evidence, and witnesses who remember Bembenek talking about how much better her life would be if Christine were "blown away."

Bembenek made license plates at 80¢ an hour in prison until 1990, when she escaped and fled to Canada with her then-fiancé Dominic Gugliatto, the brother of a fellow inmate. Her supporters wore "Run, Bambi, Run" T-shirts during her three months on the loose. She was captured after TV's *America's Most Wanted* ran her picture.

Bembenek was released in December 1993, after her new lawyer struck an agreement: her first-degree murder conviction was vacated, she pleaded no contest to second-degree murder with a 20-year sentence reduced to time served. The motivation for the deal was a 147-page legal brief that raised concerns about a sloppy police investigation and discrepancies in physical evidence. The brief also included testimony from five forensic experts that the gun presented at Bembenek's trial could not have been the murder weapon.

To this day, Bembenek's attorney claims that the case facts strongly suggest that Fred Schultz hired a hit man to kill his ex-wife. Bembenek herself believes that police let her take the fall to derail her sex-discrimination complaint from her brief stint with the Milwaukee PD.

She will be on parole until 2002.

Two TV-movies were made. 1992's *Calendar Girl, Cop, Killer? The Bambi Bembenek Story* and NBC's 1993 miniseries, *Woman on the Run: The Lawrencia Bembenek Story*, starring Tatum O'Neal, were based on Bembenek's 1992 autobiography, *Woman on Trial*.

THE SCENES:

Christine Schultz's House
19th and Ramsey
(SW side of Milwaukee)
Milwaukee, WI

Taycheedah Correctional Institute
751 Highway K
Taycheedah, WI

* * * * * *

THE STORY: *"Uneaten Remains of 11 Young Men Found in Apartment"—1991*

In 1978, Jeffrey Lionel Dahmer spontaneously killed his first victim, a hitchhiker, in Bath, Ohio. In 1982, he moved to his grandmother's home in West Allis, a suburb of Milwaukee. Five years later, young boys began to disappear. In 1988, Dahmer's grandmother asked him to leave because she couldn't stand his odd hours and the stench left from his "experiments."

The killing spree continued, with a short interruption while Dahmer served ten months for sexual assault. After his release, Dahmer moved to the **apartment building on North 25th Street** on May 14, 1990, and resumed his deadly "experiments."

A year later, on May 26, 1991, Milwaukee police caught up with one of Dahmer's victims, a Laotian immigrant named Konerak Sinthasomphone, who was naked, dazed, and bleeding in the street after escaping from the killer. Since Dahmer seemed calmer and spoke better English than the victim, they returned the doomed man to Dahmer's neat but malodorous apartment, where Sinthasomphone was promptly killed after the police left.

Four more young men died before Tracy Edwards escaped on July 22 and flagged down a patrol car with handcuffs still dangling from his wrist. While searching Dahmer's apartment, police found the dissected remains of eleven victims, including a human head in the refrigerator, human hands in a cooking pot, three more heads in a freezer, and five skulls in a box and filing cabinet. In the basement, they found a 55-gallon drum filled with chemicals and the remains of three bodies. They also found Dahmer's primary butchering tool: a chain saw.

Dahmer was convicted of murdering 15 young men and sent to the **Columbia Correctional Institute** in Portage. In jail, Dahmer amused himself by telling other inmates, "I bite," and posting notices for Cannibals Anonymous meetings.

Dahmer was murdered in prison on November 28, 1994, by Christopher Scarver, a convicted killer who'd been taking insufficient dosages of anti-psychotic medication.

THE SCENES:

Jeffrey Dahmer's Apartment
Oxford Apartments
924 North 25th Street
Apartment #213
Milwaukee, WI

Columbia Correctional Institute
2925 Columbia Drive
Portage, WI

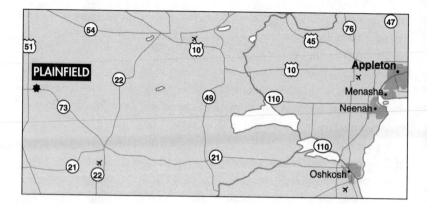

PLAINFIELD

THE STORY: *"Police Discover Death Farm, Clothes Made from People"—1957*

On November 17, 1957, Plainfield police were at Ed Gein's broken-down farmhouse questioning the peculiar loner about the disappearance of local hardware storeowner Bernice Worden. Stepping into Gein's dark, garbage-filled kitchen, a police officer brushed up against Worden's gutted body hanging upside-down from the ceiling like a dressed deer.

In addition to preserved female body parts in a shoebox, a human head, four noses, and a heart, investigators would ultimately find a grotesque collection of items made from people, including a bowl made from the top of a human skull, an armchair, lampshades, and a wastebasket made from human skin, a belt made of nipples, and, finally, a complete suit made of human skin. They finally knew what had happened to the women who'd disappeared from the area since the 1940s.

Author Robert Bloch happened to be living in a nearby town and heard about Gein. His novel about Norman Bates—based loosely on Gein—and Alfred Hitchcock's film version of the book *Psycho* changed the bathing habits of generations. To this day, millions of people are afraid to take a shower.

In addition to *Psycho*, Gein was also the inspiration for Tobe Hooper's 1974 cult film *Texas Chainsaw Massacre* and the "Buffalo Bill" character who was making a dress out of women in 1991's *The Silence of the Lambs.*

After attracting hundreds of gawkers, Gein's farmhouse "mysteriously" burned down in the early morning of March 20, 1958. Police suspected arson, but no one was ever arrested.

Gein spent ten years in the **Central State Hospital for the Criminally Insane** before ever going to trial. At the trial, people learned that in addition to murder, Gein robbed graves to get the body parts for his projects. He was quickly convicted of murder but the sentence was later reversed when it was determined that he was not guilty by reason of insanity. Gein was returned to the hospital, where he died on July 26, 1984, after a long bout with cancer. He was buried in **Plainfield Cemetery** next to his mother, near the graves that he'd robbed years earlier.

THE SCENES:

Ed Gein Held For Questioning
Wautoma County Jailhouse
   (now home of Wautoma
   Historical Society)
221 South St. Marie Street
Wautoma, WI 54982

**Central State Hospital
(now Dodge Correctional Institution)**
1 West Lincoln Street
Waupun, WI 53963

Ed Gein's Grave
Plainfield Cemetery
On Fifth Avenue, one mile
   west of town
Plainfield, WI

Wyoming

Wyoming? When it comes to crime scenes, WY-not?

The Equality State has certainly been good to historical and contemporary criminals alike. The state has provided a base of operations for Butch Cassidy's Wild Bunch and a place for more modern crimes against families too.

CHEYENNE

THE STORY: *"Teenager Ambushes, Kills Abusive Father"—1982*

 For years, IRS agent and avid gun collector Richard C. Jahnke beat his wife, son, and daughter. The senior Jahnke had few friends and rarely socialized with neighbors or co-workers. In May 1982, unable to take the abuse any longer, his son, 16-year-old Richard J. Jahnke, confided in his high school ROTC instructor, which led to a sheriff's investigation that only enraged Jahnke senior.

On November 16, as the parents left to celebrate their 20th anniversary, Jahnke ordered his son to be moved out of the house by the time he returned. In the next hour and a half, Richard and his sister Deborah prepared for war. They loaded guns and placed them around the house. Deborah was positioned in the living room with a rifle while Richard hid in the garage with a shotgun.

As the elder Jahnke approached the garage door entrance to the house, Richard fired two shotgun blasts into his 38-year-old father, and then he fired four more shots into the man's body on the floor.

In February 1983, a jury deliberated seven hours before declaring Jahnke guilty of voluntary manslaughter in the death of his father. Citing the extreme cruelty he'd experienced, Jahnke's 5 to 15 year sentence was reduced to three years by Governor Ed Herschler.

After *60 Minutes* profiled the case, a viewer wrote that Governor Herschler should be shot for letting a killer go free. Herschler's Spirit-of-the-West reply was read on the air: "My attorney tells me I can't write you a letter and call you a son of a bitch. But I can call you a son of a bitch on the telephone. What's your phone number?"

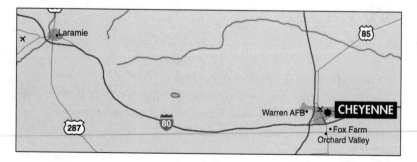

THE SCENE:

Central High School
5500 Education Drive
Cheyenne, WY 82009
307-771-2680

* * * * * *

THE STORY: *"Legendary Cowboy Hanged for Boy's Murder. But Did He Do It?"—1901*

Tom Horn, a former tracker and Army scout who participated in the capture of the Apache chief Geronimo, was a world champion steer roper, Pinkerton detective, and psychopathic hit man who died a controversial legend on both sides of the law.

Horn became a law enforcement legend after he went into Hole In the Wall and single-handedly captured notorious bank robber Peg-Leg Watson by walking right up to him and relieving him of the cocked six-guns he was aiming at Horn. Not a shot was fired. The laconic Horn later said Watson "didn't give me too much trouble."

After he tracked down and killed an estimated 17 criminals, Horn's personality began to change toward the psychopathic. He left the Pinkerton agency and became a hired gun for the Wyoming Cattle Growers' Association. When he wasn't killing rustlers, he was threatening (and murdering) the sheep ranchers and homesteaders the cattlemen wanted moved off adjacent lands.

Instead of facing his victims, Horn preferred to drop them with a powerful rifle from hundreds of yards away. His signature was a large rock left under the people he'd killed. Horn's story came to an end with the killing of Willie Nickell. According to the evidence presented at the trial, on the morning of July 18, 1901, on the Powder River Road near Cheyenne, Horn lay in wait for rancher Kels P. Nickell. Unfortunately, Nickell's tall 14-year-old son Willie picked that day to wear his father's coat and hat. As he jumped down to unlatch a gate, he was struck in the back and head with high-powered rifle bullets.

The method of the murder made Horn an immediate suspect. But there was no hard proof linking him to the murder. Joe LeFors, a Western crime-fighting legend, got Horn drunk at the **Marshall's office** and coerced a confession. Deputies in the next room witnessed the "confession" with a crude listening device.

LeFors is referred to in the movie *Butch Cassidy and The Sundance Kid*. A member of the mysterious posse wears LeFors' trademark white straw boater. LeFors arrested Horn for the killing and returned him to Cheyenne where he was later tried and hanged on a custom-built gallows. The gallows is on display at the Wyoming Frontier Prison in Rawlins.

Horn was the last man to be hanged in the state.

Despite the conviction, Horn's guilt is still disputed to this day. In 1993, Horn's retrial made front-page headlines in Cheyenne for over a week. (He was acquitted this time.)

There have been many books and two full-length movies about his life, the latest featuring Steve McQueen in one of his last film appearances.

Horn's body is buried in the Columbia Cemetery in Boulder, Colorado.

THE SCENES:

Tom Horn Memorabilia
City-County Building (site of the former courthouse where Tom Horn was held, tried and hanged.)
310 West 19th Street
Cheyenne, WY

For more information:
Cheyenne Area Convention & Visitor Bureau
307-778-3133

Marshall's Office where Horn "Confessed"
The "Commercial Block" Building (a former federal building)
The Marshall's office was on the second floor, with a bay window.
The top of the building says "Commercial Block."
Lincolnway and 16th Street
Cheyenne, WY

Willie Nickell's Grave
Lakeview Cemetery
2501 Seymour Avenue
Cheyenne, WY

Wyoming Territorial Prison and Old West Park
975 Snowy Range Road
Laramie, WY 82070
800-845-2287
Fax: 307-745-8620
prison@lariat.org
www.wyoprisonpark.org

When Butch Cassidy wasn't out robbing banks, he was doing time here at the Wyoming Territorial Prison. Check out his cell. The prison museum is now the home of the National U.S. Marshals Museum. They tamed the West, now check out the men and women who wear the star.

Be On the LookOut (BOLO): Serial Killer Alert!

The Rawlins, Wyoming, "Rodeo Murders": Four teenage girls disappeared without a trace from crowds at the Rawlins fairgrounds in July and August of 1974.

Nine years later, one of the victim's skeletons was found in Sinclair. Forensic pathologists determined that two blows to the skull had killed her. Attempts to link the killing to Ted Bundy were unsuccessful. Despite intensive police work, no signs of the other women have been found and the killer remains at large.

INDEX